D1616750

Paid Off $10,000!

"We've paid off over $10,000 this year using your tips! Should be debt free in 2020! Love you guys! Thanks for all you do!" -Lindsey

Groceries $300 A Month For Six People!

"I have learned how to save lots of money at the grocery store. Have dropped my food bill from $600 a month to $300 a month for six people. I am slowly but surely getting all my medical bills and credit cards paid off. I live on $1088 a month, so if I can do it, anyone can." -Rhonda

Spending $35 A Week!

"I have learned so much from you guys, but my favorite thing that has gone such a long way has been buying when on sale and in season! I went from spending $100-$150 a WEEK on groceries for two people (one a child)!!!! Now spending about $35-$40 a week while living in Orange County, Ca. Love what you guys do and thank you for making us get it together!!!" -Angela

Paid Off Their Car!

"Thanks to all your tips and strategies my hubby and I were able to pay off our car loan 11 months early! I made the final payment while watching your 20th Anniversary Show today. Yippie!!! Now on to the next!" -Jennifer

Best Meatloaf Ever!

"I just tried your meatloaf recipe and omg it's soo good! Who would have thought to put milk and quick oats! And "Catsup" on top only! I normally put it in! The "catsup" is like icing on the meatloaf! I also make your sweet potato casserole. So yummy with the marshmallows." -Becca

Staying Motivated!

"Never been taught to cook, never wanted to cook even. I used your tips to just get up for 5 minutes and do something. I did kept me motivated did over 10 things. I can't believe that I even want a cookbook more than I ever wanted yours... seriously... You all are very motivational and down to earth and real." -Denise

Would Have Starved Without Dining On A Dime!

"I have loved your books since the beginning and I think I we would have starved without them. I continue to use them at least four to five times a week looking up a recipe from either the books and/or the email you send out. I especially am grateful that you, your husband and your mother have helped single mothers out there to get by and strive. Thanks again and God Bless." -Sarah

Cooking Transformation!

"Generally, I'm an AWFUL cook - But Dining On A Dime has changed that! Every recipe I've tried has been delicious... I can't believe how much money I've been saving on groceries."

"Thanks again for publishing Dining on a Dime! I can't believe how much I'm enjoying cooking and my family is no longer afraid to come to the table."
-Jeannie

Can't Put It Down!

"Dining On A Dime is my absolute favorite!

I am going on a cottage vacation in the next couple of weeks and I am taking your cookbook with me.

I have never taken a cookbook on a vacation. At least I am not sleeping with it yet... hehehehe" -Deb

Better Than Betty Crocker!

"OH MY GOSH this is exactly the book I have been looking for! I have loads of cook books from expensive recipes to Amish style cooking and this one is my FAVORITE!!! Better than Betty Crocker. I recommend this book to EVERYONE I know. I WON'T dare go without my Dining On A Dime cookbook!" -A Blog Reader

Kids Love It Too!

"I just want to say a BIG thank you for making this WONDERFUL cookbook its exactly what I was looking for. I am teaching my teen age daughter to cook with this book. Thank you so much!" -Michelle

One Of The Best All-Around Cookbooks!

"We've worked with cookbook authors for 25 years and this is one of the best all around books we've ever seen. There is something here for everyone - the most amazing item is the author's list of tips for saving over $10,000 in one year - without clipping coupons or depriving your family of nutritious food.

She's an savvy shopper, a practiced cook, a clever house keeper and a creative mother who knows how to entertain her kids while teaching them excellent life skills. The price of this book will be recovered with one trip to the supermarket.

Using just a few of her ideas will make a huge impact on anyone's shrinking budget and put time back into busy days. There is an index of recipes, another index of tips, and a third index for using leftovers. Creative, entertaining, well researched and practical - this is a book you will use every day." -Merikay Jones, Cookbook Publisher

You'll Love It!

"If you like the Tightwad Gazette Books, you'll love Dining On A Dime." -Kim Tilley, Editor, Frugal Moms Newsletter

Best Brownies Ever!

"I have NEVER, in my 70 years of life (!), made brownies from scratch until I saw your recipe in cookbook I brought from you. They are absolutely delicious!

I only had one cup of flour life here at home and we wanted something sweet. My husband said he wished we had a box of brownie mix. I didn't. So I looked in your book worried that it would take a lot of flour. And voila! There it was. YOUR recipe. They came out better than boxed. I frosted them from scratch too!

Your cookbook has saved us in so so many ways. I've always thought myself a good cook and a frugal one... but frugal just got better, as did our meals and options... thanks to both of you. AND I have made so many egg rolls through this, too, thanks to me watching Mike making them awhile back. I figured if HE could do it, so could I.

I just can't thank you guys enough. But I DO say it every day as I cook from your book. Thank you again! -Janice

Might Not Have Made It!

"I am now a stay at home mom to our three children still at home and living off my husband's income alone. Thanks to your tips, tricks, and teachings we have gotten by while my husband was in school on around $2,200/month for the past 2 months with $1,450 of that per month going to rent. I can't thank you both enough. I am set to only spend $240 on groceries for the entire month of November and these last few days of October. From my family to yours THANK YOU for every time you've hit that counter and said to get it together, we may not have made it through if it wasn't for you!" -Denise

Paid Off $80,000 And Growing Rich!

"You all basically taught me how to be frugal and save money. I have purchased 2 of your books and an online course. My husband and I were $80,000 in debt. We paid it all off in 24 months on one income...plus side hustles. My husband is active duty. I am veteran that left the Army to be a stay at home mom. We are now debt free...aside from our mortgage and we have a 6 figure net worth...and we are still frugal!

Thanks for all that you do! Growing Rich, -Deedra

Dining On A Dime
Cookbook
Volume 2

1st Printing: September 2020
2nd Printing: August 2021
3rd Printing: June 2022

ISBN: 978-1-7341350-2-2

Designed, Produced and Published by:
Kellam Media and Publishing, Inc.
P.O. Box 6837
Sheridan, WY 82801

editor@livingonadime.com

Printed in Korea

Anecdotes are author unknown unless specified.

Graphics by David Kellam, the best middle child ever. Thanks, Dave!

About The Authors

Tawra Kellam and Jill Cooper are a mother-daughter team who share their recipes and tips for saving money at LivingOnADime.com.

As a single mother of two, Jill started her own business without any capital and paid off $35,000 of debt in 5 years on $1,000 a month income.

She then raised two teenagers alone on $500 a month income after becoming disabled with Chronic Fatigue Syndrome.

In five years, Tawra and her husband, Mike, paid off $20,000 of personal debt at a time when their average income was $22,000 per year.

Tawra, inspired by her mom's ways to stretch money beyond what anyone would think possible, decided to write the first edition of the Dining On A Dime Cookbook in 1997 under the title Not Just Beans.

Dining On A Dime Cookbook, Volume 1 has been in continuous publication since its first edition in 1999, with over 500,000 books sold. Tawra and Jill are known worldwide for their easy recipes and for getting dinner on the table without a lot of hassle.

Using the recipes and tips in Dining On A Dime Cookbook, Volume 1, hundreds of thousands of people have saved thousands of dollars each on their grocery bills and are living less stressful lives, thanks to Tawra and Jill's tips.

This book, Dining On A Dime Cookbook, Volume 2 includes more of the quick and easy classic money saving recipes readers have come to love!

Table Of Contents

Basics

5 Tips To Make Dinner Faster

Always do prep work ahead of time for your meal when you can. You are more likely to make dinner at the end of a long day if you have everything ready:

- **Veggies** for the meal already cleaned and cut
- **Meat** cooking in the oven or crockpot (or at least thawed)
- **Ingredients** set out and ready to toss together
- **Pan of water** on the stove, ready to cook potatoes or pasta
- **Pre-cooked meats** like hamburger, cooked and ready to use

You aren't as tempted to go out to eat if things are mostly prepared.

Make meals that will have leftovers to use for a second meal. This way you will only need to cook 3-4 nights a week instead of 7.

For example:

1st night: Chili
2nd night: Baked potatoes topped with chili or chili dogs

1st night: Roast and potatoes
2nd night: Hot roast beef sandwiches

To save money and time, keep your menus simple. More ingredients means more expensive dishes.

Serve only a few dishes. You don't need an 8 course meal every night.

Keep your recipes simple. A fresh sliced tomato can taste just as delicious with a little salt or sugar sprinkled on it as a large tossed salad.

Meal Planning Made Easy

To make meal planning much easier, have a theme for each night.

For example:

- **Monday -** Italian (spaghetti, lasagna, pizza)

- **Tuesday -** Casserole

- **Wednesday -** Mexican (tacos, quesadillas, taco salad)

- **Thursday -** Leftovers

- **Friday -** Go out to eat or have an "every man for himself" night, where each person makes what he or she wants.

- **Saturday -** Soup or stew (In the summer, you could grill instead.)

- **Sunday -** Crockpot

You can add more categories to fit your own personal tastes and switch the days around. For example, you might choose to go out to eat on Sunday and have a crockpot meal on Friday.

> When all else fails, keep calm and order pizza. DON'T YOU DARE!! You are paying off your debt and we just told you how to make easy meals. Hehehe!

Crockpot Conversions

Low	High
7 hours	3 hours
8 hours	4 hours
9 hours	5 hours
10 hours	6 hours
11 hours	7 hours
12 hours	8 hours

To convert crockpot cooking instructions to oven:

Low setting on crockpot = 190° in oven.
High setting on crockpot = 300° in oven.

How To Halve A Recipe

Recipe Calls For	To Halve
¾ cup	6 Tbsp.
⅔ cup	⅓ cup
½ cup	¼ cup
⅓ cup	2 Tbsp. plus 2 tsp.
¼ cup	2 Tbsp.
1 Tbsp.	1½ tsp.
1 tsp.	½ tsp.
½ tsp.	¼ tsp.

> I am at the "What can I make with green beans and cake mix?" stage of needing groceries.

When Fruits And Vegetable Are In Season

Winter	Spring	Summer	Fall
Apples	Apricots	Bell peppers	Apples
Beets	Artichokes	Blackberries	Beets
Bok choy	Arugula	Blueberries	Broccoli
Brussels sprouts	Asparagus	Butter beans	Brussels sprouts
Broccoli	Beets	Cantaloupe	Cabbage
Carrots	Bok choy	Corn	Carrots
Cauliflower	Broccoli	Cucumbers	Cauliflower
Celery	Celery	Eggplant	Celery
Chard	Cabbage	Figs	Collard greens
Collard greens	Green onions	Grapes	Pumpkins
Grapefruit	Kale	Green beans	Rutabagas
Kale	Peas	Honeydew	Sweet potatoes
Leeks	Radishes	Hot peppers	Tomatoes
Lemons	Rhubarb	Okra	Turnips
Lettuce	Spinach	Peaches	Winter squash
Onions	Squash	Pears	
Oranges	Snow peas	Plums	
Parsnips	Strawberries	Raspberries	
Potatoes	Zucchini	Squash	
Pumpkins		Tomatoes	
Rutabagas		Sweet potatoes	
Spinach		Watermelon	
Sweet potatoes		Zucchini	
Turnips			
Winter squash			

How To Store Your Groceries

Fruits	Where To Store	How To Store	How Long It Keeps
Apples	refrigerator drawer	unwrapped	Up to 10 weeks
Avocado	countertop until ripened/ refrigerator shelf when ripe	unwrapped	4 days after ripe
Avocado (halved)	refrigerator	lemon squeezed on flesh, wrapped in plastic	1 day
Banana	countertop	unwrapped, still in peel	3 days after ripe
Banana (halved)	refrigerator	foil wrapped on cut end	1-2 days
Berries	refrigerator drawer	vented container	3-5 days
Citrus	refrigerator drawer		2 weeks
Citrus (halved)	refrigerator drawer	wrapped in plastic	2-3 days
Grapes	refrigerator drawer	perforated plastic bag	1-2 weeks
Melon	countertop	whole	5 days after ripe
Melon (halved)	refrigerator shelf	wrapped in plastic	7-10 days
Peaches Plums Pears	countertop to ripen refrigerator shelf when ripe		4-5 days after ripe

Vegetables	Where To Store	How To Store	How Long It Keeps
Asparagus	refrigerator	stems in water, plastic bag over tops	4 days
Beets	refrigerator	plastic bag	2 weeks
Bell pepper	refrigerator	plastic bag	1 week
Broccoli	refrigerator	wrapped in plastic	5 days
Cabbage	refrigerator	wrapped in plastic	2-3 weeks
Carrots	refrigerator	plastic bag	1 month
Cauliflower	refrigerator	wrapped in plastic	5 days
Celery	refrigerator	wrapped in foil	2 weeks
Cucumbers	refrigerator		1 week
Dark leafy greens	refrigerator	plastic bag with dry paper towel	1 week
Garlic	dark pantry	unwrapped whole	2 months
Ginger	refrigerator	unwrapped	1 month
Ginger (cut)	refrigerator	plastic bag with dry paper towel	1-2 weeks
Green beans	refrigerator	plastic bag with dry paper towel	1 week
Head of lettuce	refrigerator	plastic bag with dry paper towel	5 days
Mushrooms	refrigerator	paper bag	3 days
Onions	dark pantry	unwrapped	1-2 months
Onions (halved)	refrigerator	plastic bag	3-5 days
Parsnips	refrigerator	plastic bag	2 weeks
Potatoes	dark pantry	paper bag	1-2 months

Vegetables	Where To Store	How To Store	How Long It Keeps
Radishes	refrigerator	plastic bag with dry paper towel	2 weeks
Salad greens	refrigerator	large plastic container layered with dry paper towels	10 days
Summer squash	refrigerator	plastic bag	5 days
Sweet potatoes	dark pantry	paper bag	2 weeks
Tomatoes	countertop		5 days
Winter squash	dark pantry		1 month
Winter squash (halved)	refrigerator	wrapped in foil	2-3 weeks

Herbs	Where To Store	How To Store	How Long It Keeps
Basil	countertop	stems in water, lightly covered with plastic	1 week
Chives	refrigerator	wrapped in damp paper towel in a plastic bag	5 days
Cilantro	refrigerator	stems in water, lightly covered with plastic	1 week
Parsley	refrigerator	stems in water, lightly covered with plastic	1 week
Rosemary/ Thyme	refrigerator	wrapped in plastic	2 weeks

Meats/Fish/Eggs	Where To Store	How To Store	How Long It Keeps
Bacon	refrigerator/ meat drawer	sealed bag unsealed bag	2 weeks unopened, 1 week opened
Bacon	freezer	sealed bag	1 month
Cold cuts (from the deli)	refrigerator	2 weeks unopened	5 days, opened
Cold cuts	refrigerator	package they came in	2 weeks unopened, 5 days opened
Eggs	refrigerator	egg carton	2 weeks or until expiration date
Live shellfish	refrigerator	shallow tray in single layer covered with damp paper towel	1 day
Raw fish	refrigerator	package it came in	1 day
Raw fish	freezer	sealed bag	3-6 months
Smoked fish	refrigerator	sealed bag unsealed bag	2 weeks unopened, 5 days opened
Smoked fish	freezer	sealed bag	6 months
Raw meat	refrigerator	package it came in	2 days
Raw meat	freezer	sealed bag	3-6 months
Poultry	refrigerator	package came in	2 days
Poultry	freezer	sealed bag	3-6 months

Bread/Dairy	Where To Store	How To Store	How Long It Keeps
Bread	counter	sealed bag	5-7 days
Bread	freezer	sealed bag	3-6 months
Cheese, fresh (mozzarella, etc.)	refrigerator	in water/change every 2 days	1 week
Cheese, soft	refrigerator	plastic	1-2 weeks
Cheese, semi hard	refrigerator	plastic	2 weeks
Cheese, hard aged	refrigerator	plastic	1 month
Most cheeses	freezer	plastic bag	3-6 months

Miscellaneous	Where To Store	How To Store	How Long It Keeps
Baking powder	cool, dry place	original container	1 year
Beans	cool, dry place	bag	forever
Chocolate chips long term	cool, dry place freezer	bag bag	1 year 1 year
Coffee	cool, dry place	original container	5 years
Flour long term bug prone areas	cool, dry place freezer freeze 24 hours, then cabinet	bag	1 year 1 year 1 year
Honey	cool, dry place	original container	20 years
Nuts long term	cool, dry place freezer	bag bag	6 months 1 year
Oils	cool, dry place	original container	1 year
Rice	cool, dry place	bag	5 years
Sugar, brown	cool, dry place	bag	5 years
Sugar, granulated	cool, dry place	bag	5 years
Sugar, powdered	cool, dry place	bag	5 years
Tea	cool, dry place	original container	20 years

How To Freeze

If you think you will need longer term freezer storage (over 4-6 months), you can use a vacuum sealer to package items in vacuum sealed bags.

Apples
Make and freeze in small usable portions. Lay items flat to store in the freezer, like:
 Applesauce
 Apple butter
 Apple pie filling

Avocado
 Mash avocado and add desired seasonings. Add ¼ tsp. (minimum) lemon or lime juice for each avocado. Place in small sandwich bags, lay flat and freeze. Defrost and enjoy!

Bacon
 Uncooked: Freeze in the package from the store.
 Cooked: Freeze in freezer bags.

Bananas
 Baking: Freeze ripe bananas whole in skin. To use in breads, let defrost for 15 minutes. Remove top, squeeze out banana, all smashed and ready to go.
 Smoothies and ice creams: Peel bananas straight out of the freezer and use.

Berries
 Freeze on trays in a single layer. When frozen, put in freezer bags. Alternatively, just dump them straight into a freezer bag and whack the bag on the counter to break them apart when needed.

Bread
 Freeze loaves of bread whole in the package up to 2 months.

Broth
 Make broth and freeze in freezer bags in 2 cup portions. Lay flat to store in freezer.

Butter
 Put butter straight into the freezer as-is.

Cheese
Shredded: Freeze in the bags it comes in.

Blocks: Freeze and defrost before using.

Chicken, cooked
Put in freezer bags in meal-sized portions. Lay flat.

Coffee
Put coffee grounds in smaller, usable amounts in bags with all the air squeezed out. Pull out coffee, defrost and use.

Eggs, whole
Beat eggs until blended. Put in freezer bags. Defrost in the refrigerator or in water. Use only in baked goods.

Flour
Leave in package and freeze overnight to kill weevils. Store in a sealed container in the pantry.

For longer storage, place flour in the freezer in freezer bags.

Garlic
Easy peel garlic: Put garlic cloves into a container. Close and shake vigorously until the cloves separate and the peels come off.

Remove peels. Chop. Mix with 2 Tbsp. oil for each cup of garlic. Place on a cookie sheet in a thin layer and freeze. When frozen, break into pieces and put into a freezer bag.

Hamburger
Cook and drain. Freeze into meal-sized portions, usually ½ to 1 pound each. Put in fold top sandwich bags and freeze in a larger freezer bag.

Herbs
Chop. Put in silicone ice cube trays, fill with water and freeze. Transfer to freezer bags when frozen. Use in cooked food.

Lemons
Slices: Freeze in ice cube trays with water for drinks.

Peels: Freeze peels on a tray. When frozen, place in freezer bags.

Milk
Freeze in the plastic jugs. Remove ½ cup before freezing if there is no indentation on the side of the jug.

Oranges

Whole oranges: Don't freeze well.

Orange juice: Place in freezer bags and lay flat.

Orange juice in plastic jugs: If it has an indentation on the side of the jug, put straight into freezer. If no indentation, pour ½ cup off; then freeze.

Onions

Slice/chop into desired pieces. Dump into a freezer bag and freeze*.

You can also place on a cookie sheet in a single layer and freeze. Then place into freezer bags. Use only in cooked foods.

*I use the dump method but, if you do, the onions stick together in the freezer bag. When I need to use them, I whack the bag on the counter. Then the pieces break off and I use what I need.

Pies

Filling: Pour into freezer bags. Lay flat in the freezer and freeze.

Whole: Freeze pies WITHOUT meringue, whole, wrapped in plastic wrap.

Nuts

Freeze in the bags they come in.

Tomatoes

Place tomatoes whole in freezer bags.

To use: Take out of the freezer and let defrost about 30 minutes. The skins will fall right off. Chop or grind into the desired consistency. Use in chilis and soups.

Salsa

Fill freezer bags with salsa. Defrost, drain off excess liquid and use. (Save excess liquid for chili.)

Soups

Pour soup into freezer bags in meal-sized portions. Lay flat and freeze.

Sweet Potato

Cook and remove from skin. Place in freezer bags and lay flat.

Wine

Freeze in ice cube trays for cooking. Store cubes in a freezer bag.

Substitutions

Cheese

Cream cheese	=	cottage cheese, blended smooth with butter or milk
Romano	=	Parmesan
Ricotta	=	cottage cheese

Eggs

1 egg	=	1 Tbsp. soy flour and 1 Tbsp. water

Flour

1 cup sifted cake flour	=	1 cup less 2 Tbsp. sifted all purpose flour
1 Tbsp. cornstarch	=	2 Tbsp. flour for thickening sauces and gravies

Sugar

1 cup granulated sugar	=	1¾ cups powdered sugar or 1 cup packed light brown sugar or ¾ cup honey
1 cup powdered or confectioner's sugar	=	½ cup plus 1 Tbsp. granulated sugar
1 cup brown sugar	=	1 cup sugar plus 2 Tbsp. molasses

Substitutions

Milk/Cream

1 cup milk	=	⅓ cup dry milk plus 1 cup water or ½ cup evaporated milk plus ½ cup water
1 cup buttermilk	=	1 cup plain yogurt or 1 Tbsp. lemon juice or vinegar plus enough milk to make 1 cup. Let stand 5 minutes.
1 cup heavy cream or half and half	=	⅞ cup whole milk plus 3 Tbsp. butter
1 cup light cream	=	⅞ cup whole milk plus 1½ Tbsp. butter
1 cup sour cream (for baking)	=	1 cup plain yogurt
1 cup sour milk	=	1 cup plain yogurt or 1 Tbsp. lemon juice or vinegar plus enough milk to make 1 cup
1 cup whole milk	=	1 cup skim milk plus 2 Tbsp. butter or margarine

Substitutions

Miscellaneous

1 pkg. active dry yeast	=	½ cake compressed yeast or 1 Tbsp. bulk yeast
1 tsp. baking powder	=	¼ tsp. cream of tartar plus ¼ tsp. baking soda
1 Tbsp. lemon juice	=	½ Tbsp. vinegar
1 cup chopped apples	=	1 cup chopped pears plus 1 Tbsp. lemon juice
1 cup dry bread crumbs	=	¾ cup cracker crumbs or 1 cup corn flake crumbs
1 cup butter	=	1 cup margarine or ⅞ cup vegetable oil
1 Tbsp. cornstarch	=	2 Tbsp. all purpose flour
1 cup dark corn syrup	=	¾ cup light corn syrup plus ¼ cup light molasses
1 chopped onion	=	1 Tbsp. instant minced onion
1 clove garlic	=	¼ tsp. garlic powder
1 cup tomato sauce	=	½ cup tomato paste plus ½ cup water
1 Tbsp. prepared mustard	=	1 tsp. dry mustard plus 1 Tbsp. water
1 tsp. dried herbs	=	1 Tbsp. fresh herbs
1 ounce unsweetened chocolate	=	3 Tbsp. unsweetened cocoa powder plus 1 Tbsp. butter, margarine or shortening

Healthy Substitutions For Recipes

Instead Of	Use
Bacon	Smoke flavoring, ham, Canadian bacon or bacon bits
Bread crumbs	French bread, dried and crushed
Butter, margarine or shortening in baking	Applesauce
Cream cheese	Neufchatel or low fat cream cheese
Canned condensed soup	White sauce made with skim milk
Cream of chicken soup	1¼ cups white sauce + 1 Tbsp. chicken bouillon
Cream of mushroom soup	1 cup white sauce + 1 can drained mushrooms
Egg (one)	2 egg whites
Ground beef	Ground turkey
Heavy cream, for whipping	Evaporated milk, freeze 30 min. Add ½ tsp. vanilla, whip
Heavy cream, in sauces and soups	Evaporated milk
Ricotta cheese	Low fat cottage cheese, pureed
Sour cream	Yogurt
Whole milk	Skim milk
White flour	½ white and ½ wheat
White flour, for thickening	2 Tbsp. cornstarch
White rice	Brown rice

Equivalents

3 teaspoons	=	1 tablespoon
4 tablespoons	=	¼ cup
16 tablespoons	=	1 cup
1 gallon	=	4 quarts
	=	8 pints
	=	16 cups
	=	128 fluid ounces
1 quart	=	2 pints
	=	4 cups
	=	32 fluid ounces
1 pint	=	2 cups
	=	16 fluid ounces
1 gill	=	½ cup
	=	4 fluid ounces
	=	8 tablespoons
1 fluid ounce	=	2 tablespoons
1 tablespoon	=	½ fluid ounce
	=	3 teaspoons

To convert **ounces** to **grams,** multiply ounces x 28.35

To convert **pounds** to **grams,** multiply pounds x 453.59

To convert **Fahrenheit degrees** to **Celsius degrees**:
$$°C = (°F-32) \times 5/9$$

1 stick butter = **8** tablespoons = **4** ounces = ¼ pound

High Altitude Adjustments

Don't assume recipes won't work at high altitudes. Many of these recipes have been tested successfully in altitudes up to 8,000 feet above sea level. I suggest making a recipe first to see how it turns out before adjusting it.

Deep Fat Frying - Lower the temperature 3° for every 1,000 feet above sea level to keep from burning the food.

Adjustments For Cakes:

3,000-5,000 feet:

Reduce baking powder: for each teaspoon, decrease ⅛ teaspoon.
Reduce sugar: for each cup, decrease 0 to 1 tablespoon.
Increase liquid: for each cup, add 1 to 2 tablespoons.
Increase oven temperature by 25°.

5,000-7,000 feet:

Reduce baking powder: for each teaspoon, decrease ⅛ to ¼ teaspoon.
Reduce sugar: for each cup, decrease 0 to 2 tablespoons.
Increase liquid: for each cup, add 2 to 4 tablespoons.
Increase oven temperature by 25°.

Adjustment for 7,000+ feet:

Reduce baking powder: for each teaspoon, decrease ¼ teaspoon.
Reduce sugar: for each cup, decrease 1 to 3 tablespoons.
Increase liquid: for each cup, add 3 to 4 tablespoons.
Increase oven temperature by 25°.

Candy Making - decrease final temperature 2° for every 1,000 feet above sea level.

Yeast breads - 2 risings may be needed. Once doubled in size, punch down and let it rise again.

Cookies - Decrease flour and increase baking temperature slightly. Most cookies work at high altitudes.

Notes

Beverages

1 Step Refrigerator Tea
Safe Sun Tea

Do you remember Sun Tea? Well the bad news is it's not very good for you because it can grow harmful bacteria. The good news is you can make refrigerator tea at home for pennies and still have the great flavor that sun tea had.

4   tea bags
4   cups water

Fill a pitcher or mason jar with water. Hang tea bags in the water. Cover and steep 6-12 hours in the refrigerator. Serve as desired with any flavorings or sweeteners.

Peach Tea

1   cup sugar
1   cup water
2-3 fresh peaches, sliced (You can use blueberries, blackberries, strawberries or raspberries.)
6   cups brewed tea

Place sugar, water and peaches into a saucepan and cook until they come to a boil. Reduce heat to a simmer. Crush the peaches as you stir to dissolve the sugar. Once the sugar is dissolved, turn off the burner, cover, and allow the mixture to rest for about 30 minutes.

Strain the syrup to remove the fruit pieces. Save the fruit pieces for smoothies. Add the syrup to the tea and refrigerate. Serve over ice.

Easy Flavored Tea

3   family size tea bags
4   flavored tea bags (lemon, blueberry, blackberry, mint, orange,
        cinnamon-- any flavor will work.)
1   cup sugar

Place tea bags and sugar in a gallon pitcher with a lid. Pour 4 cups boiling water over tea bags. Steep for 6 minutes. Press and squeeze remaining tea out of bags and remove tea bags. Stir until sugar is dissolved. Add cold water and ice to fill.

Citrus Tea

6   cups boiling water
2   regular individual size tea bags
6   Tbsp. sugar or honey
1   stick cinnamon
    juice of 2 lemons
    slices of orange, lemon, lime and/or cucumber

Place tea bags, sugar, and cinnamon stick in a 2 quart pitcher. Pour water over everything. Cover and let rest for 1 hour. Discard the cinnamon stick. Stir in lemon juice. Add sliced fruits. Refrigerate overnight or until chilled. Add ice cubes and slices of citrus before serving.

• **Freeze small amounts of juice or the juices from your canned fruit like pineapple and peaches in ice cube trays. You can use these cubes to flavor teas or in place of water in your Jello. The frozen cubes will help the Jello set up more quickly than water.**

Starbucks® Mocha Copycat

Coffee

2	Tbsp. chocolate syrup
2	oz. espresso or strong coffee
1	cup milk, steamed
	whipped cream

Layer ingredients, starting with the chocolate syrup, then espresso and then steamed milk. Top with whipped cream and additional chocolate syrup.

Variation

Caramel Mocha: Add 2 tablespoons caramel syrup plus the chocolate syrup. (Other coffee flavors may be used if you like.)

- **Keep a couple of ice cube trays in the freezer and, when you have leftover coffee, tea or even chocolate milk, add it to the trays and freeze. Then you'll have ice cubes for your iced coffee, tea or for an extra cool glass of chocolate milk.**

Caramel Frappuccino® Copycat

2   cups ice
¼   cup strong brewed coffee, cooled
1   cup milk
¼-½ cup caramel sauce (to taste)
3   Tbsp. sugar
        whipped cream, optional

Blend ingredients together until smooth. Top with whipped cream, if desired. Serves 2.

Mocha Frappuccino® Copycat

2   cups ice
¼   cup strong brewed coffee, cooled
1   cup milk
⅓-½ cup chocolate sauce (to taste)
1   tsp. vanilla
3   Tbsp. sugar
        whipped cream, optional

Blend ingredients together until smooth. Top with whipped cream, if desired. Serves 2.

• **Bitter coffee? Add a pinch of salt and a pinch of cinnamon to your coffee grounds before brewing.**

Pumpkin Pie Latte

5 cups strong coffee
4 cups milk
½ cup heavy whipping cream
¼ cup pumpkin, canned or roasted (not pumpkin pie mix)
⅓ cup sugar
1 tsp. vanilla
1 tsp. pumpkin pie spice
  whipped cream
  cinnamon stick (optional)

Mix ingredients in a crockpot and cook on high for 2 hours, stirring after 1 hour. Serve topped with whipped cream and a cinnamon stick (optional).

Coffee Hot Chocolate Mix

2 cups powdered non-dairy coffee creamer
1½ cups instant hot chocolate mix
1½ cups instant coffee granules
1½ cups sugar
1 tsp. cinnamon
½ tsp. nutmeg

Mix ingredients and store in a container. When ready to make, mix 1 cup hot water and 2 heaping tablespoons of mix.

French Vanilla Cocoa Mix

6   cups powdered milk
2   cups powdered sugar
1   (8 oz.) container French vanilla non-dairy coffee creamer
2   cups Nesquik
1   (6 oz.) box instant French vanilla pudding mix

Mix all ingredients and store in an airtight container or put in Mason jars for gifts.

Attach this note to the jar for gifts:

Mix 3 tablespoons of mix with one cup hot water. Stir until mixed.

Peppermint White Hot Chocolate

4   cups milk or 4 cups half and half or a combination of the two
8   oz. white chocolate, chopped (or white chocolate chips)
1   tsp. vanilla
½   tsp. peppermint extract (to taste)

Optional Toppings

whipped cream
crushed peppermints
marshmallows

Stir the milk and white chocolate together in a medium saucepan. Cook over medium-low heat, stirring occasionally, until the mixture comes to a simmer and the chocolate is melted. (Do not let it come to a boil or let the chocolate burn on the bottom.) Remove from heat; stir in vanilla and peppermint extract.

Milkshakes

Make these milkshakes green for St. Patrick's Day, red for Christmas or Valentine's Day or any color to match your child's birthday party.

2   cups vanilla ice cream*
¾   cup milk
      food coloring

In a blender, blend the ice cream and milk. Then add food coloring. You can make a batch of pink, then one of blue, and finally purple and slowly pour some of each into a glass. Top with whipped cream and sprinkles.

*Any flavor ice cream may be used.

Pineapple Smoothie

This smoothie is cool for a hot August day and not too sweet. Don't let the buttermilk scare you.

1½   cups unsweetened pineapple juice
1   cup buttermilk
2   cups ice cubes
2   (8 oz.) cans crushed pineapple
¼   cup sugar

Mix everything in a blender until smooth. Serve immediately.

Strawberry Cheesecake Smoothie

1	cup frozen strawberries
¾	cup plain Greek yogurt or vanilla ice cream
½	cup milk
2	oz. cream cheese
1	Tbsp. vanilla
2	Tbsp. sugar

Place all ingredients in a blender and blend until smooth. Serve immediately.

Strawberry Lemonade Slushies

1	packet lemonade flavored drink mix (Kool-Aid*)
½	cup sugar (or more, to taste)
2	cups seltzer or club soda
5	large strawberries, stems removed
2½	cups ice

Place all ingredients in a blender. Pulse until ice is finely crushed. Serve immediately.

*Any flavor of Kool-Aid will work for different flavor combinations.

Italian Cream Soda

2-4 Tbsp. raspberry syrup (or any other flavor)
1   cup club soda or sparkling water
2-4 Tbsp. heavy whipping cream

Fill a tall glass halfway with crushed ice. Add syrup and then carbonated water. Top with half and half and then stir and enjoy!

Mock Champagne Punch

1   qt. white grape juice, chilled
1   qt. ginger ale, chilled
     strawberries and/or raspberries

Combine juice and ginger ale. Garnish with berries. Makes 16 half cup servings.

This can be doubled, tripled or quadrupled for your parties.

• **When making your favorite fruit punch, add a package of unsweetened lemonade flavored drink mix to it for an extra kick.**

Eggnog

(Non-Alcoholic)

6	lg. egg yolks
½	cup sugar
1	cup heavy whipping cream
2	cups milk
½	tsp. nutmeg
	pinch of salt
¼	tsp. vanilla
	cinnamon (for topping)

Whisk egg yolks and sugar together in a medium bowl until light and creamy.

In a saucepan over medium-high heat, combine the cream, milk, nutmeg and salt. Stir often, until mixture barely simmers.

Add a big spoonful of the hot milk to the egg mixture, whisking vigorously. Repeat, adding a big spoonful at a time, to temper the eggs. (Temper means warming the eggs without cooking them.)

Once most of the hot milk has been added to the eggs, pour the mixture back into the saucepan on the stove.

Whisk constantly for just a few minutes, until the mixture is just slightly thickened (or until it reaches about 160° on a thermometer). It will thicken more as it cools.

Remove from heat and stir in vanilla. Pour the eggnog into a pitcher or other container and cover with plastic wrap. Refrigerate until chilled. It will thicken as it cools.

If you want a thinner, completely smooth consistency, you can add the entire mixture to a blender with 1 or 2 tablespoons of milk and blend until smooth.

Serve with a sprinkle of cinnamon, and fresh whipped cream, if desired.

Store homemade eggnog in the fridge for up to one week.

Hot Spiced Drink Mix

2   lbs. brown sugar
5½   Tbsp. pumpkin pie spice mix

Whisk together and store in an airtight container or put in Mason jars for gifts.

Attach this note to the jar for gifts:

For 1 cup: Use 1 Tbsp. mix with 1 cup apple cider. Steep 5 minutes.

For 4 cups: Use ¼ cup mix with 4 cups cider. Steep 5 minutes.

Variations

- **In place of cider,** add to tea, coffee, hot orange juice or other juice.

- **For a pot of coffee,** add ¼ cup of mix to the brew basket.

- **For cranberry cider,** use 3 cups apple cider, 1 cup cranberry juice cocktail, and ¼ cup spice mix.

- **Don't like the taste of tap water? Pour your water into a jug and put it in the refrigerator overnight. All of the chlorine and chemical taste disappears and the water is delicious.**

French Vanilla Creamer

2   cups milk
1   (14 oz.) can sweetened condensed milk
2   tsp. vanilla

Mix all ingredients in a quart jar. Shake until well blended.

Variations

- **Cappuccino:** Add 1 tsp. almond extract and ½ tsp. orange extract
- **Amaretto:** Add ½ tsp. cinnamon and 1 tsp. almond extract
- Add flavored syrups for additional flavors, to taste

Chocolate Almond Creamer

2   cups milk
1   (14 oz.) can sweetened condensed milk
1   tsp. almond extract
1   Tbsp. cocoa

Mix all ingredients in a jar. Shake until well blended.

Coconut Coffee Creamer

1   cup high-fat canned coconut milk*
1   Tbsp. vanilla
     sweetener (to taste)

Mix and store in the refrigerator. Add 1-2 tablespoons to each cup of coffee.

Coconut coffee creamer can be stored in the refrigerator for 10-14 days.

Be sure to shake well before using because coconut milk is so thick it needs to be mixed well to distribute properly.

*Sometimes called coconut cream

Coconut Almond Coffee Creamer

1   (13 oz.) can coconut milk
2   Tbsp. almond milk
3   Tbsp. sugar
     pinch salt
½   tsp. vanilla

Pour everything except vanilla into a saucepan and stir to combine. Cook over medium-low heat until sugar is dissolved. DO NOT BOIL!

Remove from heat and add vanilla. Cool.

Store in a glass jar in the refrigerator. Shake before serving.

Notes

Breakfast

Breakfast Tips

Uses for bacon grease - Bacon grease is free. Most of us could spend 50% less on oils and save if we just started using our bacon grease.

To store - Cool in pan. When cooled, but still liquid, strain and pour into a jar with a lid. Store in refrigerator.

Use bacon grease for cooking:

- Fried eggs
- Scrambled eggs
- French toast or pancakes
- Country fries
- Hash browns
- Drizzle a little on warm potatoes for potato salad.
- Cooking pork chops
- Cooking hamburger
- Lightly rub on bread dough to keep dough from drying out while rising.
- Use melted bacon grease in place of oil in waffles recipe
- Use 1 teaspoon or so in green beans for flavor.
- Drizzle on veggies before roasting them.

- **If leftover muffins are a little dry,** scoop out the centers and add some jam with a dot of butter. If they are savory muffins, add a little grated cheese. Warm them up and watch them disappear.

- **To know when a griddle is hot enough,** drop a couple of drops of water on it. If the griddle is ready, it will crackle and pop when the water drops touch it.

- **When having a pancake brunch,** mix your pancake batter and freeze it in quart size bags. The night before you need the batter, place it in the fridge to thaw overnight. The next day, just clip a small corner of the bag and pour the desired amount for each pancake on the skillet. No messy clean up.

Eggs

How To Tell If Eggs Are Bad

Fill a bowl with cold water and place your eggs in the bowl.

Very fresh eggs - Sink to the bottom of the bowl and lay flat on their sides.

Few weeks old but good to eat - Stand on one end at the bottom of the bowl.

Bad - Float to the top.

How to Cook Eggs Over Easy

Heat butter or bacon grease in a nonstick skillet over medium-high heat until it's hot and foamy. Break eggs and gently slide into pan, one at a time. Reduce heat to low immediately. Cook slowly until whites are slightly firm, but yolks are still runny. Carefully slide a spatula under each egg and flip. Cook until the eggs reach desired doneness. Serve.

Over medium: Yolks begin to thicken (only slightly runny) but not hard.

How To Boil Eggs

Soft-boiled eggs: 4 minutes

Slightly soft-boiled eggs: 5 minutes

Custardy yet firm soft-boiled eggs: 6 minutes

Creamy hard-boiled eggs: 7 minutes

Firm yet still creamy hard-boiled eggs: 8 minutes

Very firm hard boiled eggs: 10-11 minutes

High Altitude: add 2-3 minutes

Storage: Refrigerate any unused hard boiled eggs, still in their shells. They can be stored in the refrigerator for up to 1 week. Mark shell with permanent marker to identify hard boiled eggs in the fridge.

Prevent Eggs From Cracking

Use room temperature eggs to make boiled eggs. Don't place the cold eggs from the fridge into the hot water on the stove. Place the eggs in cold water and then turn on the cooktop. If an egg has a crack, you can add a little bit of vinegar to the pot. The vinegar will help to congeal the egg white if it starts to leak out from the shell.

Easy To Peel Hard Boiled Eggs

- **Use older eggs** (1 week old). Eggs that are a few days old are easier to peel.

- **Add ½ tsp salt** to the water. Adding salt to the water may help make the eggs easier to peel.

- **Add ½ tsp baking soda.** Some people suggest adding baking soda to the water, which increases the alkalinity of the water and makes the eggs easy to peel.

- **Add vinegar** (if you are using farm fresh eggs). You can easily peel hard boiled eggs by adding a little bit of vinegar to the water while boiling, which makes the shells softer.

- **Roll eggs on the counter.** After boiling the eggs, cool in ice cold water. Roll them on the counter to remove the shells. The shells will fall off easily.

- **Run under water.** Crack eggs all around without peeling them and place them under a little bit of running water or soak in a bowl of water for a while. The water penetrates under the shell and makes them easier to peel.

Bacon In The Oven

Preheat oven to 400°. Line baking sheet with foil, if desired, for easy cleanup. Arrange bacon slices in a single layer. Bake 18-22 minutes, until crispy.

Optional: You can place a metal baking rack on a baking sheet to drain bacon grease away from the bacon while cooking.

Bacon In The Microwave

Line a microwave safe plate with two paper towels. Lay bacon on paper towels in one layer. Cover with an additional paper towel. Microwave 4-5 minutes. Check the bacon and continue to cook in 30 second to one minute increments. It usually takes around 7 minutes total, depending on your microwave.

Total time bacon took to cook in my microwave: _____

Billion Dollar Idea

A smoke detector that shuts off when you yell, "I'm just cooking."

Oatmeal

Servings	1	2	3
quick cooking oatmeal	½ cup	1 cup	1½ cups
water	1 cup	1¾ cups	2½ cups
salt	pinch	⅛ tsp.	⅛ tsp.

Stovetop

Boil water and salt. Stir in oats. Cook 1 minute over medium heat, stirring occasionally.

Microwave

Combine water, salt and oats in a medium microwave safe bowl. Microwave on high for 1½-2 minutes. Stir before serving.

Instant Oatmeal Packets

½	cup quick oats
⅛	tsp. salt
½	Tbsp. sugar (brown or white)
1	Tbsp. oat flour (optional)*
½	Tbsp. dry powdered milk (optional)**
⅛	tsp. cinnamon
	mix-ins like raisins, dried fruit, etc.

Put all ingredients in a zip top bag.

To serve, pour into a bowl, add ¾ cup water and microwave 1-2 minutes. Serves 1.

*Oats blended in blender. Makes a thicker oatmeal.

**Makes a creamier oatmeal.

Steel Cut Oats

3   cups water
1   cup milk
1   Tbsp. butter or margarine
1   cup steel cut oats*
¼   tsp. salt
    optional mix-ins: cinnamon, dried fruits, nuts, lemon or
      orange zest

In a large saucepan, combine water, milk and butter. Bring the mixture to a simmer over medium heat.

Stir in the oats. Reduce the heat to medium-low and simmer gently for about 20 minutes, stirring occasionally, until the mixture is very thick.

Add salt. Continue to simmer mixture, stirring occasionally until almost all of the liquid is absorbed, about 10 minutes. The oatmeal will be very creamy when it's done.

Remove from heat and stir in any mix-ins that you'd like. Let the oatmeal rest for 5 minutes before serving so it has more time to thicken.

*To toast oatmeal (optional): Melt butter or margarine in a 12 inch skillet over medium heat. Once shimmering, add the oats and cook, stirring occasionally, until golden and fragrant, around 2 minutes. This toasting step greatly enhances the flavor of the oats.

• **When you have two glasses stuck together, don't force them apart. Instead, fill the inside glass with cold water and set the bottom in hot water at the same time. The bottom glass will slightly expand and the inside one will contract, allowing them to separate.**

Baked Oatmeal

1½   cups quick cooking oats
½   cup sugar
½   cup milk
¼   cup butter or margarine, melted
1   large egg
1   tsp. baking powder
¾   tsp. salt
1   tsp. vanilla
      warm milk
      fresh fruit and/or brown sugar (optional)

Preheat oven to 350°. Combine the first eight ingredients. Mix well. Spread evenly in a greased 9x13 inch baking pan. Bake 25-30 minutes or until edges are golden brown. Immediately spoon into bowls and add milk. Top with fruit and/or brown sugar if desired.

Cornmeal Pancakes

1⅓   cups all purpose flour
⅔   cup cornmeal
2   Tbsp. sugar
4   tsp. baking powder
1   tsp. salt
2   large eggs
1⅓   cups milk
¼   cup butter or margarine, melted

Combine ingredients in the order listed. Stir, just until moistened. Pour batter by ¼ cupfuls onto a lightly greased hot griddle. Turn when bubbles on top begin to pop. Cook until second side is golden brown. Serve with syrup.

Apple Cider Pancakes

Make the syrup for this recipe first
so everything is ready at the same time.

¾	cup all purpose flour
2	tsp. sugar
¼	tsp. baking soda
¼	tsp. salt
¼	tsp. cinnamon
⅔	cup apple, peeled and finely chopped
¼	cup raisins
⅔	cup buttermilk
1	large egg, separated
2	tsp. butter or margarine, melted
¼	tsp. vanilla

In a small bowl, combine the first five ingredients. Stir in apple and raisins. Add buttermilk, egg yolk, butter and vanilla. Stir into dry ingredients. In a small bowl, beat egg white until soft peaks form. Fold into batter.

Pour batter by heaping ¼ cupfuls onto a hot griddle coated with cooking spray. Turn when bubbles form on top. Cook until the second side is lightly browned.

Serve pancakes with warm syrup and, if desired, additional butter.

Apple Cider Syrup

¼	cup sugar
2	tsp. cornstarch
⅔	cup apple cider or juice
1	cinnamon stick
	dash nutmeg

In a small saucepan, combine the sugar, cornstarch and cider until smooth. Add cinnamon stick. Bring to a boil over medium heat. Cook and stir for 2 minutes or until thickened. Discard cinnamon stick. Stir nutmeg into syrup.

German Pancake

6   large eggs
1   cup milk
1   cup all purpose flour
½   tsp. salt
2   Tbsp. butter or margarine, melted

Preheat oven to 400°. Place first four ingredients in a bowl. Whisk just until smooth.

Add butter into a 9x13 inch baking dish. Place in oven to melt. When melted, tilt dish to coat. Add batter. Bake, uncovered, until puffed and golden brown, about 20 minutes.

While pancake is baking, make the caramel syrup (below).

Remove pancake from oven. Dust with powdered sugar. Serve immediately with syrup and, if desired, fresh blueberries.

Caramel Syrup

½   cup butter
1½   cups sugar
¾   cup buttermilk
2   Tbsp. corn syrup
1   tsp. baking soda
2   tsp. vanilla
      powdered sugar
      fresh blueberries (optional)

Place butter, sugar, buttermilk, corn syrup and baking soda into a small saucepan. Bring to a boil. Cook, uncovered, for 7 minutes. Remove from heat. Stir in vanilla.

French Toast Sticks
This is the BEST French Toast I've ever eaten!

8	slices bread (Texas Toast or French style)
¼	cup butter or margarine, melted
4	eggs
⅓	cup sugar
¼	tsp. cinnamon
⅔	cup milk
¾	tsp. vanilla

Preheat oven to 350°. Cut each slice of bread into 3 pieces to make sticks. In a bowl, mix together melted butter, eggs, sugar, cinnamon, milk and vanilla. Beat well.

Spray a cookie sheet with cooking spray. Dip bread sticks into egg mixture and place on cookie sheet. If there is any egg mixture left, you can drizzle it over the sticks. Bake for 25 minutes on middle oven rack. Turn halfway through baking time.

To freeze: Allow to cool. Freeze on a cookie sheet. As soon as it is frozen, remove and place in a Ziploc bag.

To reheat: Place 3 sticks in microwave and heat on high for 1 minute, until warm. Serve with syrup.

Women's Magazines:

Page 14: You are beautiful the way you are.

Page 15: How to lose weight fast.

Page 16: Cake recipe.

Overnight Baked French Toast

12	slices French bread (1 inch thick)
8	large eggs
2	cups milk
2	tsp. vanilla
½	tsp. cinnamon
¾	cup butter or margarine, softened
1⅓	cups brown sugar, packed
3	Tbsp. dark corn syrup
1	cup walnuts or pecans, chopped

Place bread in a greased 9x13 inch baking dish. In a large bowl, beat eggs, milk, vanilla and cinnamon. Pour over the bread. Cover and refrigerate overnight. Remove from the refrigerator 30 minutes before baking.

After removing baking dish from the refrigerator, in a separate bowl, cream butter or margarine, brown sugar and corn syrup until smooth. Spread over bread. Sprinkle with nuts.

Bake, uncovered, at 350° for 1 hour or until golden brown.

Just spent 15 minutes looking for my phone in my car while using my phone as a flashlight.

Stuffed French Toast

2	eggs
½	cup milk
½	tsp. sugar
½	tsp. cinnamon
¼	tsp. vanilla
1	(8 oz.) pkg. cream cheese
12	slices white bread
⅓	cup strawberry jam
	butter or margarine, for cooking
	maple syrup, for serving (optional)
	strawberry syrup (optional)
	confectioners' sugar, for serving (optional)

In a small bowl, whisk together the eggs, milk, sugar, cinnamon and vanilla. Spread the cream cheese on half of the bread slices and top with jam. Top with the remaining 6 bread slices and press around the edges to seal into sandwiches.

Melt butter or margarine on a griddle over medium-low heat. Dip the sandwiches in the egg mixture for a few seconds on each side. Cook the sandwiches until golden brown, 2 to 3 minutes per side. Serve with maple syrup, strawberry syrup, or confectioners' sugar.

Strawberry Syrup

3	cups mashed strawberries
1	cup sugar
1½	tsp. lemon juice

In a medium saucepan, combine all the ingredients and bring to a boil. Lower the heat and simmer until the strawberries are soft and the syrup is thickened and reduced by ⅓-½ of the volume, about 15-18 minutes. Remove from the heat and let cool to room temperature before serving.

Apple Cider Donuts

2   cups apple cider
3½   cups all purpose flour
⅔   cup brown sugar, packed
2   tsp. baking powder
¾   tsp. salt
½   tsp. baking soda
¼   tsp. nutmeg
¼   tsp. cinnamon
¼   tsp. allspice
2   large eggs, room temperature
6   Tbsp. butter or margarine, melted and cooled
      oil for frying
      vanilla glaze (p. 277) (optional)

In a small saucepan, bring cider to a rapid boil. Cook over medium heat until reduced by half, about 12 minutes. Cool completely.

Whisk together dry ingredients. Add cider, eggs and butter or margarine to dry ingredients and mix, just until moistened (dough will be sticky). Refrigerate, covered, until firm enough to shape, about 1 hour.

Divide dough in half. On a floured surface, pat each portion to ½ inch thickness. Cut with a floured 3 inch donut cutter.

Donuts: In a skillet or deep fryer, heat oil to 325°. Fry donuts, a few at a time, until golden brown, about 2-3 minutes on each side.

Donut holes: Fry a few at time, until golden brown and cooked through, about 1 minute on each side.

Drain on paper towels. Cool slightly. If desired, dip donuts into glaze or sugar of your choice.

1 Muffin 22 Variations

1   egg
½   cup milk
¼   cup vegetable oil
1½ cups all purpose flour
½   cup sugar
2   tsp. baking powder
½   tsp. salt

Preheat oven to 400°. Grease muffin cups or use muffin liners. Mix together egg, milk and oil. Add flour, sugar, baking powder and salt. Mix until just moistened. THE BATTER SHOULD BE LUMPY. DO NOT OVER MIX.

Fill muffin cups ⅔ full. Bake 20 to 25 minutes, until golden brown. Serve warm.

Variations

Jumbo Muffins: 425° for 5 minutes. Then reduce to 350° for 22-25 minutes, for a total of 27-30 minutes. Makes about 6.

Mini Muffins: 350° for 12-14 minutes. Makes about 36-40.

Apple Cinnamon Muffins: Add ½ tsp. cinnamon, ¼ tsp. nutmeg, 1 cup peeled chopped apple and ½ cup chopped pecans or walnuts into the batter. Sprinkle muffin tops with some oats before baking.

Banana Nut Muffins: Add ¾ cup mashed banana and 1 cup chopped walnuts. Cream cheese frosting would be delicious on these!

Bacon or Ham Muffins: Reduce sugar to 2 Tbsp. and add ½ cup chopped bacon or ham.

Birthday Cake Muffins: Add ¾ cup rainbow sprinkles to muffin batter. Optional: Add 1 tsp. almond extract.

Blueberry Muffins: Mix 1 cup blueberries into the batter. After baking, drizzle with lemon glaze. (For lemon glaze, add 1 tsp. lemon juice to vanilla glaze.)

Blueberry Lemon Muffins: Add zest and juice of 1 lemon and 1½ cups fresh or frozen blueberries to muffin batter.

Cheese Muffins: Add ½ cup grated cheese and ⅛ tsp. paprika.

Cherry Or Cranberry Muffins: Mix ⅔ cup cherries or cranberries with 2 Tbsp. sugar. Add to batter and bake.

Chocolate Chip Muffins: Fold ¾ cup semi-sweet chocolate chips into the muffin batter.

Cinnamon Pecan Muffins: Add ¾ cups toasted chopped pecans and ¾ cup cinnamon chips to muffin batter.

Cornmeal Muffins: Use ½ cup cornmeal and 1 cup all purpose flour in place of 1½ cups all purpose flour.

Cranberry Apple Muffins: Add 1 cup peeled chopped apple and ¾ cup fresh or frozen cranberries to muffin batter.

Dried Fruit Muffins: Add ½ cup dried apricots, currants, peaches, figs, prunes, raisins or dates to muffin batter.

Ginger Peach Muffins: Add 1¼ cups peeled and chopped peaches and 2 Tbsp. freshly grated ginger.

Lemon Poppy Seed Muffins: Mix 2 Tbsp. poppy seeds with zest and juice from 2 medium lemons into the muffin batter. Sprinkle muffin tops with coarse sugar before baking. After baking, drizzle with lemon glaze. (For lemon glaze, add 1 tsp. lemon juice to vanilla glaze.)

Nut Muffins: Add ⅓ cup chopped nuts to muffin batter.

Pear Spice Muffins: Add 1¼ cups peeled chopped pear and ¼ tsp. each nutmeg, ground cloves and allspice to muffin batter.

Pineapple Coconut Muffins: Add 1 cup sweetened shredded coconut and ¾ cup finely chopped pineapple (fresh or canned) to the batter.

White Chocolate Raspberry Muffins: Fold 1 cup raspberries and ¾ cup white chocolate chips into the muffin batter.

Whole Wheat: Replace 1 cup all purpose flour with whole wheat flour.

Jammy Donut Muffins

1¾ cups all purpose flour
1½ tsp. baking powder
½   tsp. salt
½   tsp. nutmeg
¼   tsp. cinnamon
¾   cup sugar
⅓   cup canola oil
1   large egg, lightly beaten
¾   cup milk
10 tsp. seedless strawberry or other jam

Topping

¼   cup butter or margarine, melted
⅓   cup sugar
1   tsp. cinnamon

Preheat oven to 350°. In a large bowl combine flour, baking powder, salt, nutmeg, cinnamon and sugar. Stir until combined. Add oil, egg and milk. Stir into dry ingredients just until moistened.

Fill greased or paper-lined muffin cups half full. Place 1 teaspoon jam in each muffin cup. Cover jam with enough batter to fill muffin cups ¾ full. Bake 20-25 minutes or until a toothpick comes out clean.

Place melted butter in a small bowl. Combine sugar and cinnamon in another bowl. Immediately after removing muffins from the oven, dip tops in butter, then in cinnamon sugar. Serve warm.

Blueberry Coffee Cake Muffins

¾	cup butter or margarine, room temperature
1½	cups sugar
3	eggs
1½	tsp. vanilla
1	cup sour cream
¼	cup milk
2	tsp. baking powder
½	tsp. baking soda
½	tsp. salt
2½	cups all purpose flour
1	pint fresh blueberries*

Preheat oven to 350°. Place paper liners in muffin pans.

In a bowl, cream the butter and sugar until light and fluffy, about 5 minutes. Add eggs, one at a time. Then add vanilla, sour cream, milk, baking powder, baking soda and salt. Mix batter on low speed. Add flour and mix, just until combined. Fold in blueberries and mix. Be sure the batter is completely mixed.

Fill each muffin cup ⅔ full, and bake 25 to 30 minutes, until the muffins are lightly brown and a cake tester comes out clean.

*You can leave out blueberries for plain muffins or add any other mix-ins you like from pages 64-65 (22 variation pages), such as chocolate chips.

Some days I amaze myself. Other days
I put my keys in the refrigerator.

Blueberry Streusel Coffee Cake

¾   cup sugar
½   cup butter or margarine, softened
1   egg, room temperature
½   cup milk
2   tsp. baking powder
¼   tsp. salt
2   cups all purpose flour
1   cup fresh or frozen blueberries
1   cup pecans, chopped

Streusel Topping

½   cup sugar
⅓   cup all purpose flour
¼   cup cold butter or margarine

Preheat oven to 375°. In a bowl, cream sugar and butter until light and fluffy. Add egg and milk. Stir in baking powder, salt and flour. Fold in blueberries and pecans. Spread into a greased 9 inch square baking pan.

For topping, combine sugar and flour. Cut in butter until crumbly. Sprinkle over batter. Bake until a toothpick inserted in the center comes out clean, about 35-40 minutes. Cool on a wire rack.

You only live once..... lick the bowl.

Easy Cheese Danish

1	(8 oz.) pkg. cream cheese, room temperature
⅓	cup sugar
2	egg yolks, room temperature
2	Tbsp. ricotta cheese
1	tsp. vanilla
¼	tsp. salt
2	sheets (1 pkg.) frozen puff pastry, defrosted
1	egg beaten with 1 Tbsp. water (for egg wash)

Grease a sheet pan or line with parchment paper.

Cream together cream cheese and sugar together until smooth. Add egg yolks, ricotta cheese, vanilla and salt. Mix until just combined.

Don't whip!

Unfold 1 sheet of puff pastry onto a lightly floured board. Roll slightly with a floured rolling pin into a 10x10 inch square. Cut into quarters.

Place a heaping tablespoon of cheese filling into the middle of each of the 4 squares. Brush the border of each pastry with egg wash and fold 2 opposite corners to the center, brushing and overlapping the corners of each pastry so they firmly stick together. Brush the tops with egg wash.

Place pastries on sheet pan. Repeat with the second sheet of puff pastry. Refrigerate filled danish for
15 minutes.

Preheat oven to 400°. Bake about 20 minutes, rotating the pan once during baking, until puffed and brown. Serve warm.

Biscuits And Gravy

Serve biscuits separate from gravy. To eat, pour gravy over biscuits.

Baking Powder Biscuits

2   cups all purpose flour
3   tsp. baking powder
1   tsp. salt
5   Tbsp. butter or margarine
1   scant cup milk

Preheat oven to 425°. Mix flour, baking powder and salt in a bowl. Cut in butter or margarine with a fork or pastry blender until it resembles cornmeal. Add milk, stirring enough to combine ingredients. Do not over-stir. Put dough on a lightly floured surface and gather into a ball. If the dough is sticky, add a little flour to help form the ball.

Knead lightly 5-10 times. Roll out ½ inch thick and cut with a biscuit cutter or a glass rim that has been dipped in flour. Put onto an ungreased cookie sheet and bake 15-20 minutes or until golden brown. Makes 10-12 biscuits.

Sausage Gravy

1   roll breakfast sausage
2-4 Tbsp. sausage drippings (grease)*
4   Tbsp. all purpose flour
2   cups milk
     salt and pepper (to taste)

Cook sausage. Leave 2-4 tablespoons of drippings (and crumbs) in the pan, draining the rest. Add flour to the drippings. Quickly whisk to mix and loosen the crumbs. The mixture will be thick. Slowly add milk, whisking to mix into the flour mix. Whisk well. Bring to a boil, whisking the whole time until mixture is thick. If it gets too thick, add a little more milk. Salt and pepper to taste.

*If you don't have 2-4 tablespoons of grease leftover from frying, just add butter, margarine, oil or bacon grease to get that amount.

Avocado Toast

1   slice bread (Thick sliced bread is best.)
½   ripe avocado
      pinch salt

Toast bread until golden and firm. Mash avocado with a fork until it is as smooth as you like it. Add salt, to taste. Spread on toast. Then top with desired toppings.

Toppings

- **Garlic:** Add a sprinkle of garlic powder or ½ tsp. crushed garlic to avocado.

- **Herbed:** Add some chopped fresh basil, cilantro, dill or parsley to avocado.

- **Pesto**

- **Egg:** Add a poached egg or scrambled egg on top.

- **Pickled onions**

- **Pickled jalapeños**

- **Sliced cherry tomatoes** or sun dried tomatoes

- **Everything Bagel Avocado Toast**
  Add a sprinkle of everything bagel seasoning (p. 350) on top of your avocado toast.

- **Cafe Style Avocado Toast**
  Spread a thick layer of mashed avocado over your toast. Then drizzle with 1 tsp. olive oil, 1 tsp. lemon juice, a generous sprinkle of red pepper flakes and flaky salt.

Breakfast Skillet

4	slices bacon, cut into 1 inch pieces
1	onion, chopped
3	russet potatoes, chopped into ¾ inch cubes
¼	cup water
2	cloves garlic, minced or 2 tsp. minced garlic
1	onion, diced
½	tsp. smoked paprika
	salt (to taste)
	pepper (to taste)
4	eggs or Polish sausage, diced*
1	cup Cheddar cheese, shredded

Cook bacon until crispy. Remove from pan, leaving the bacon grease in the pan. Add onion, sautéing until soft. Add potatoes. Stir well. Add water and cover. Cook until potatoes are tender, about 20 minutes. Add more water if they brown too quickly.

When potatoes are tender, mix in garlic, onion, paprika, salt and pepper. Make 4 holes in potato mix to reveal bottom of pan. Crack an egg into each hole, seasoning with salt and pepper. Sprinkle cheese and bacon bits over all. Replace lid and cook until eggs are cooked to your liking, about 5 minutes for runny eggs.

*You can use either one or both.

- **If your jam or jelly doesn't set up, add a little water to it and boil. This makes great syrup.**

Breakfast Burritos

½   lb. bulk pork sausage or ½ lb. bacon
1   (16 oz.) pkg. frozen cubed hash brown potatoes
12   eggs (or ½-1 link Polish sausage, to taste)*
1   large onion, chopped
1   medium green pepper, chopped
12   flour tortillas (10 inch), warmed
3   cups Cheddar cheese, shredded
    salsa (optional)

In a large skillet, cook sausage or bacon. Drain, leaving 2 tablespoons oil from sausage in the pan. Cook hash browns according to package directions. Remove hash browns and set aside.

In a large bowl, beat eggs*. Add onion and green pepper. Pour into the same skillet. Cook and stir until eggs are set.

Remove from heat. Add hash browns and sausage. Mix gently.

Preheat oven to 350°. Place about ¾ cup filling on each tortilla and top with about ¼ cup cheese. Roll up and place on a greased baking sheet. Bake 15-20 minutes or until heated through. Serve with salsa, if desired.

*If using Polish sausage instead, of eggs, just cut the sausage in the pan and heat until warmed through.

To Freeze

Oven: Wrap in foil and freeze. Place in oven at 350° for 30 minutes to warm.

Microwave: Wrap in parchment paper and freeze. Remove from parchment paper, wrap in a wet paper towel and microwave for 3 minutes to warm.

Amish Breakfast Casserole

1	lb. bacon, diced
1	onion, chopped
6	large eggs, lightly beaten
4	cups frozen shredded hash brown potatoes, thawed
2	cups Cheddar cheese, shredded
1½	cups cottage cheese
1¼	cups Swiss cheese, shredded

Preheat oven to 350°. In a large skillet, cook bacon and onion over medium heat until bacon is very crisp*. Drain. In a large bowl, combine remaining ingredients. Stir in bacon mixture. Transfer to a greased 9x13 inch baking dish.

Bake, uncovered, until a knife inserted in the center comes out clean, 35-40 minutes. Let stand 10 minutes before cutting.

*If bacon is not very crisp, the casserole will be soggy.

I wonder what my kids are going to tell their kids... "It was so rough back then. I didn't have a phone 'til the 4th grade and the WiFi didn't always reach upstairs."

Omelet

2   eggs
     salt and pepper (to taste)
     olive oil or other cooking oil (optional)

Fillings of your choice, up to 5 Tbsp. combined:

- cheese, grated
- bacon or bacon bits
- ham or other lunch meat, sliced small
- black olives, sliced
- mushrooms, sliced
- green, white or red onion, chopped
- bell peppers or other peppers
- tomatoes, diced
- salsa
- any other meat, cheese or veggie ingredient that sounds good

Crack eggs into a measuring cup or bowl. Scramble lightly with a fork. Add salt and pepper.

Heat non-stick frying pan on medium-high heat for 2 minutes with a small amount of oil or butter. When heated, pour egg mixture into the frying pan. Watch carefully as it will cook quickly.

As the edges of the egg begin to stiffen, quickly add each of the desired filling ingredients.

When the edges of the eggs pull away from the pan slightly and the eggs are setting up in the middle, carefully slip the spatula under one side of the omelet and fold it over the other half. Reduce heat and let it cook a little more to seal the omelet closed. Continue cooking until the eggs are as cooked as you desire, flipping the omelet over after it seals if you'd like to cook the other side more.

Don't overcook or it will get dried out.

Slide the omelet out of the pan onto a plate. Garnish with remaining filling ingredients to make it pretty. Cheese, olives, onions and tomatoes make nice garnish toppings.

Serve right away.

- **If you plan to make more than one omelet, prepare all of the filling ingredients in advance.** After cooking the first omelet, remove the pan from the heat for a moment to let it cool slightly. If the pan gets too hot, the eggs will begin sticking to it and will be more difficult to turn.

- **If something goes wrong** and you don't manage to keep the omelet together while you're flipping it, you can still serve it. If you don't like how it looks, you can quickly break it up, as with scrambled eggs, and turn it into "ranchero eggs".

I'm just going to flip this omelet here annnnnnd ahhhhhh...
I am going to have scrambled eggs.

Bacon, Egg And Cheese Biscuit Bake

8   strips bacon, uncooked
4   eggs
1   can Grands Buttermilk biscuits (8 biscuits)
6   slices American cheese, quartered
2   Tbsp. butter or margarine, melted

Preheat oven to 350°. Grease a 9x13 inch pan.

In a skillet, cook bacon until crisp. Remove bacon from skillet and crumble. Drain fat from skillet, reserving 1 tablespoon fat.

In medium bowl, beat eggs with fork or whisk until well mixed. Pour egg mixture into skillet with bacon fat. Cook 3-5 minutes, stirring frequently.

Separate dough into 8 biscuits. Pull each biscuit in half. Press each half into a rectangle ½ inch thick. Place 1 tablespoon scrambled eggs, 2 teaspoons bacon and 1 piece cheese on half of each rectangle. Fold dough over mixture. (Do not seal.) Place in a baking dish in 4 rows by 4 rows.

Bake 20 to 25 minutes or until biscuits are cooked through and deep golden brown on top. Brush biscuits with 2 tablespoons melted butter.

I just did an inventory of my Tupperware:
17 round containers, 2 square lids.

Huevos Rancheros

1	Tbsp. olive oil
½	medium onion, chopped
1	(15 oz.) can crushed tomatoes (fire-roasted, if possible)
½	can or 3 oz. diced green chiles
	chipotle chili powder (optional, to taste)
	adobo sauce (optional, to taste)*
	cumin (optional, to taste)
4	corn tortillas
2	tsp. butter or margarine
4	fresh eggs
2	Tbsp. fresh cilantro, chopped (optional)

Sauté onions in olive oil over medium heat, until translucent. Add tomatoes (with their juices), green chilies and additional chili, adobo and cumin to taste. Reduce heat to low. Simmer, stirring occasionally.

Reduce to warm after simmering for 10 minutes. Add salt to taste, if needed.

In a separate pan, add butter or margarine and fry eggs the way you like them. Warm tortillas.

To serve, spoon a little of the sauce onto a warmed plate. Top with a tortilla, then a fried egg. Top with more sauce, sprinkle with cilantro if desired.

*Can be found in the Mexican food section of your grocery store.

Frittata

This is a very versatile recipe. Use any vegetables or meat.
Tomatoes, onions, peppers or bacon are good options.

6	eggs, beaten
1	oz. grated Parmesan cheese
½	tsp. pepper
	pinch salt
1	tsp. butter or margarine
½	cup asparagus, chopped and roasted
½	cup ham, chopped
1	Tbsp. parsley leaves, chopped (optional)

Preheat oven to broil setting.

In a medium-sized bowl, using a fork, blend together eggs, cheese, pepper, and salt. Heat a 12 inch non-stick, oven safe sauté pan over medium-high heat. Add butter or margarine to pan and melt. Add asparagus and ham to pan and sauté for 2 to 3 minutes.

Pour egg mixture into pan and stir. Cook for 4-5 minutes or until the egg mixture has set on the bottom and begins to set up on top.

Sprinkle with parsley. Place pan into oven and broil for 3-4 minutes, until lightly browned and fluffy. Remove from pan and cut into 6 servings. Serve immediately.

Quiche

1   cup onion, chopped
1   cup fresh mushrooms, sliced
1   Tbsp. vegetable oil
5   oz. frozen chopped spinach, thawed and well drained
⅔   cup fully cooked ham, finely chopped
5   large eggs
3   cups Muenster or Monterey Jack cheese, shredded
⅛   tsp. pepper

Preheat oven to 350°. In a large skillet, sauté onion and mushrooms in oil until tender. Add spinach and ham. Cook and stir until the excess moisture is evaporated. Cool slightly.

Beat eggs. Add cheese and mix well. Stir in spinach mixture and pepper. Blend well.

Spread evenly into a greased 9-inch pie plate or quiche dish. Bake 40-45 minutes or until a knife inserted in center comes out clean.

Spiced Bacon

¼   cup brown sugar, packed
1½   tsp. ground mustard
⅛   tsp. cinnamon
⅛   tsp. nutmeg
     dash cayenne pepper
10   pieces bacon

Preheat oven to 350°. Combine first five ingredients. Rub over bacon on both sides. Twist bacon. Place on a rack in a 15x10x1 inch baking pan. Bake 25-40 minutes, until desired firmness.

Notes

Breads

Bread Tips

- **Important note about preparing baking pans:** If a recipe calls for parchment paper or greasing a baking pan, you can interchange them or you can also choose to use a silpat.

- **One way to tell if bread is done** is to thump with your finger. If it sounds hollow then it is done.

- **Put a cooking thermometer inside bread.** If it reads 200°, it is done.

- **When a recipe says to knead on a floured board,** reserve the last ½ cup of flour the recipe calls for and use it for the kneading. This way, your bread will not become too dry from too much flour.

- **You don't have to knead bread on the counter.** You can knead it right in the bowl you mixed it in.

- **When making a loaf of bread,** you don't have to roll it out into a rectangle. You can just mold the dough into a loaf.

- **Try to have most of the ingredients for bread,** like eggs, flour, butter and margarine at room temperature.

- **To test baking powder for freshness,** place ½ tsp. into hot water. If it fizzes, it is okay.

- **To test if your yeast is fresh,** put yeast in warm water and if, after 3-5 minutes, it is bubbling and increases in size, it is fresh. If you don't see bubbles, it is not fresh and the yeast is dead.

- **If you have long fingernails,** use disposable gloves to knead dough so the dough does not get stuck under your nails.

- **When baking bread,** place a pan of 8 ice cubes on lower shelf. The steam helps make the bread come out perfect.

No Yeast Bread

4¼   cups all purpose flour
1½   tsp. salt
1½   tsp. baking soda
2   Tbsp. sugar
4   Tbsp. butter, melted
1¾   cups buttermilk, plus 1 Tbsp. for brushing the dough
1   Tbsp. whole oats and/or a sprinkle of coarse salt for topping

Preheat oven to 400°. Grease a baking sheet or line with parchment paper.

Whisk the flour, salt, baking soda and sugar together in a large bowl. Add melted butter and buttermilk. Combine. Mixture will form a loose, stiff, and slightly moist dough.

Put the dough and any flour crumbles that haven't been incorporated onto a lightly floured work surface. With floured hands, work the dough into a ball and flatten into a 7-8 inch disc, about 2 inches tall. If the dough is too sticky, add a little more flour.

Transfer to pan. Brush the top of the loaf with buttermilk. Using a very sharp knife, score a ¾ inch deep X into the top. Sprinkle optional oats and/or coarse salt on top of the loaf.

Bake until the bread is golden brown and center appears cooked through, about 45 minutes. Loosely cover the bread with aluminum foil halfway through bake time to protect the crust from over-browning before the center has a chance to cook.

Remove from the oven and allow bread to cool at least 5 minutes before slicing.

For best taste, let the bread cool for at least 30 minutes before slicing and serving.

Cover and store bread at room temperature for 3 days or in the refrigerator for up to 1 week.

90 Minute Amish Bread

5½-6 cups all purpose flour
1   Tbsp. or 1 pkg. instant yeast
⅓   cup sugar
2   tsp. salt
1½   cups water
½   cup milk
½   cup butter or margarine

Combine 2 cups flour, yeast, sugar and salt in a bowl. Stir until blended. Heat water, milk and butter until 120°-130°*. The butter does not need to melt. Add to flour mixture.

Beat 2 minutes at medium speed, scraping bowl occasionally.

Add 1 cup flour. Beat 2 minutes at high speed, scraping bowl occasionally.

Stir in just enough remaining flour so that the dough will form into a ball.

Knead in a bowl or on a lightly floured surface until it is smooth and elastic and springs back when lightly pressed with 2 fingers, about 6 to 8 minutes. Cover with a towel. Let rest for 10 minutes.

Cut dough into 2 equal pieces. Form each piece into a loaf. Place loaves, seam sides down, into two greased loaf pans. Cover with a towel. Let rise in a warm place until doubled in size, about 45 minutes.

Preheat oven to 400°. Bake 20-30 minutes or until golden brown**.

Remove from pans by running a knife around the edges and inverting bread onto a wire rack. Rub tops with butter and cool.

*Use an instant read thermometer to make sure temperature is right.

**Bread will sound hollow when tapped with a finger or when a meat thermometer inserted into the bread reads 195-200°.

Jill's Sticky Buns

1   batch Amish Bread dough (p. 88),
       using ½ cup sugar instead of ⅓ cup sugar in dough

Filling

2-4 Tbsp. butter or margarine, softened
½   cup brown sugar
1   Tbsp. cinnamon

Topping

2   cups brown sugar
¾   cup butter or margarine, melted
⅔   cup whipping cream
      nuts, chopped (optional)

After making dough, let rise until doubled.

Roll out into a rectangle. Starting with butter, spread the filling ingredients evenly over the dough.

Roll dough, jelly roll fashion. Slice into ½-1 inch thick slices. Grease two 9x13 inch pans.

Mix topping ingredients and pour half into each pan. Then sprinkle nuts on top, if using. Place the cinnamon rolls in pans. Let rise until doubled.

Preheat oven to 350º. Bake 20-25 minutes.

Cinnamon Bread

1   batch Amish Bread dough (p. 88),
       using ½ cup sugar instead of ⅓ cup sugar in dough

Filling

½   cup sugar
2   tsp. cinnamon
3-4 Tbsp. butter or margarine, softened

After making dough, place in a greased bowl, turning to grease the top. Cover and let rise in a warm place until doubled, about 15-20 minutes.

Combine sugar and cinnamon for the filling.

Punch down dough. Divide in half. Roll each half to a 14x9 inch rectangle. Brush butter on the rectangles.

Sprinkle with sugar and cinnamon mix. Starting at the 9 inch end, roll each rectangle, jelly roll fashion. Shape into loaves and place into 2 greased 9x5 inch loaf pans. Cover and let rise until doubled, about 35 minutes.

Preheat oven to 400°. Bake 20-30 minutes or until golden brown**. Remove from pans by running a knife around the edges and inverting bread onto a wire rack. Rub tops with butter and cool.

**Bread will sound hollow when tapped with a finger or when a meat thermometer inserted into the bread reads 195-200°.

• **Tip: Grease muffin tins with bacon grease. It adds a great flavor but the rolls don't taste like bacon.**

60 Minute Rolls

1   batch Amish Bread dough (p. 88)

For the first rising of the Amish Bread dough, let rise for 15 minutes.

Divide into 36 balls and place into muffin tins or on a cookie sheet. Cover and let rise 15 minutes in a warm place.

Preheat oven to 325°. Bake 12 minutes or until done.

Remove from pans. Rub butter on top and let cool.

> If you don't have time to travel to Madagascar to pick your own vanilla beans, store bought is fine.

No Knead
4 Ingredient Bread

This an easy, rustic artisan bread.

2	cups warm water (110°)
1	Tbsp. salt
1	Tbsp. or 1 pkg. yeast
4	cups all purpose flour

Mix salt, yeast and water. Stir until dissolved. Add flour. Mix until well blended. Cover in a bowl with plastic wrap, leaving a small hole in the plastic wrap. Let rise 2 hours.

Sprinkle a small amount of flour on top and punch down. Divide dough in half to make two balls, using just enough flour so you can make each into a ball. It will be sticky. Fold the edges under to form a smooth top. Let rise on parchment paper on a cookie sheet for 40-50 minutes until doubled.

Optional: Put melted butter on top with some sesame seeds. Score the top of the bread with a knife. Place an oven-safe pan with 1 cup of water in oven. (The steam this creates will give the bread a chewy, crispy crust.)

Preheat oven to 450° and bake 30 minutes.

No Knead Bread In Dutch Oven

To rise, place dough in a parchment paper lined bowl (not wax paper) and cover with a towel. Let stand on countertop for about 35 minutes.

Place Dutch oven with lid into a **cold oven** and preheat to 450°. When oven reaches 450°, carefully lift the parchment paper and dough and place gently into the hot pot. (Parchment paper goes in the pot, too.) Cover and bake 30 minutes. After 30 minutes, remove lid and parchment paper. Return, uncovered, to oven and bake 10-15 more minutes. Let it cool at least 15 minutes before slicing.

Texas Roadhouse® Rolls Copycat

These dinner rolls are just like the ones at Texas Roadhouse!

1	Tbsp. or 1 pkg. yeast
¼	cup warm water (110°)
1	cup milk
2	Tbsp. butter
¼	cup sugar
1	tsp. salt
4-4½	cups all purpose flour
1	egg

Dissolve yeast in warm water. Let stand about 5-10 minutes, until bubbly.

Combine milk and butter. Warm to about 115°, until butter starts to melt. (If you put your finger in and it is really warm but not hot, that's just right. If it is too hot, let it cool.)

Combine sugar, salt, 1 cup of flour, yeast mixture, milk and butter in a bowl. Beat thoroughly.

Add 1 cup of flour and egg and beat for 2 minutes on high. Add 2 cups of flour and stir into dough.

Lightly flour dough and knead a few times until it is soft but not sticky. (You can knead in the bowl.) Place in a greased bowl and let rise until doubled, 45 minutes to an hour.

Punch down. Turn out onto a floured board. Divide in half and then roll into a "log". Cut portions for shaping. Shape dough into rolls. Place on greased baking sheets or greased pans. Let rise until doubled.

Preheat oven to 350°. Bake 10-15 minutes, until golden brown.

As soon as you take them out of the oven, spread butter all over the tops. Serve with Texas Honey Butter (p. 335).

Sourdough Bread

If you have never made sourdough bread, it is delicious! First, you make a sourdough starter that you will use to make bread again and again. Because the starter includes active yeast, the yeast continues to grow so you don't have to add yeast to any of the bread you make using the starter.

The first time you make the starter, it will take a little longer. Once you have the starter, it is easy to keep feeding it and then making the bread is easier and takes less time. You can also save money not buying yeast every time you make bread and if yeast is in short supply, you only need to buy yeast once for many loaves of bread.

Sourdough Starter

3½   cups all purpose flour
1   Tbsp. sugar
1   Tbsp. or 1 pkg. yeast
2   cups warm water (110°)

In large bowl, combine everything, gradually adding warm water to dry ingredients. Beat until smooth. Cover with plastic wrap and let stand for 2 days in a warm place. Stir before using.

To Use: Use the amount called for in the recipe.

To Replenish starter: Add 1½ cups flour and 1 cup warm water to starter. Beat until smooth. Store in a warm place for 2 days.

If you don't use for in 1 week, discard 1½ cups starter, and follow replenishing instructions.

If you like, use discarded starter in:

pancakes
waffles
biscuits

Making The Sourdough Bread

¾ cup milk
3 Tbsp. sugar
1 tsp. salt
2 Tbsp. butter or margarine
¼ cup warm water (110°)
1 Tbsp. or 1 pkg. yeast
1½ cups sourdough starter
5-6 cups all purpose flour

Heat milk, sugar, salt and butter to lukewarm. Pour warm water into a large bowl and sprinkle with yeast, stirring to dissolve.

Add milk mixture, sourdough starter and 2½ cups flour. Beat until smooth. Stir in enough additional flour to make a stiff dough. Turn onto a lightly floured board and knead until smooth and elastic, about 8-10 minutes.

Place in a greased bowl, turning to grease the top. Cover and let rise in a warm place until doubled, about 1 hour.

Punch down, divide into 3 loaves and form each into a smooth round ball. Place on a greased baking sheet. Cut crisscross section on tops of the round loaves. Cover and let rise again until doubled, about 1 hour.

Preheat oven to 400°. Bake about 25 minutes or until done.

Remove from baking sheets and cool on wire rack. Makes 3 loaves.

Variations

For Cinnamon Bread: Roll out dough, spread butter over it and sprinkle with cinnamon and sugar. Roll up. Let rise until doubled in pan and bake.

For Cinnamon Rolls: Roll out dough, spread butter over it and sprinkle with cinnamon and sugar. Roll up and cut into slices (your desired thickness). Let rise until doubled in pan and bake.

For Cheese Bread: Knead 2 cups shredded cheese into dough. Let rise until doubled in pan and bake.

For Pizza Crust: Roll out as you would for pizza. Makes 2 pizza crusts.

No Knead Dinner Rolls

2	Tbsp. shortening
¼	cup sugar
1	cup hot water (130-140°)
1	Tbsp. or 1 pkg. yeast
1	egg
1	tsp. salt
2¼	cups all purpose flour

In a large bowl, mix shortening, sugar, and hot water. Stir to melt shortening. Allow to cool until lukewarm (110°).

Mix in the yeast until dissolved. Mix in egg, salt and flour. The dough will be VERY, VERY sticky. It's ok. Leave it in the bowl and allow the dough to rise until doubled in size.

Grease 12 muffin cups. Divide the dough into the prepared muffin cups and allow to rise again, until doubled in size.

Preheat oven to 425° and bake 10 minutes or until a knife or toothpick inserted in the center of a muffin comes out clean.

That awkward moment when you are
not actually sure you have free time
or if you're just forgetting everything.

Pull Apart Bread

¾   cup warm milk (110°)
1   Tbsp. or 1 pkg. yeast
3   Tbsp. butter or margarine
2   Tbsp. sugar
1   egg
1   tsp. salt
3   cups all purpose flour

Filling

⅔   cup brown sugar
1   tsp. cinnamon
3   Tbsp. butter or margarine, melted
1   large apple, diced

Glaze

1   cup powdered sugar
1   Tbsp. milk

In a bowl, combine milk and yeast. Let mixture stand 10 minutes, until it gets foamy. Add butter, sugar, egg and salt. Beat to combine. Add half of the flour and beat for 30 seconds. Scrape down the bowl. Beat for 3 more minutes.

Add the remaining flour. Knead to form the dough into a ball. Spray top and bottom of dough with cooking spray. Cover and let it rise until it is almost doubled in size.

Mix sugar and cinnamon for filling. Roll dough into 1½ inch balls. Roll in melted butter, then in sugar and cinnamon mix.

Place into a 9x5 inch greased loaf pan, spreading apples across and between the dough. Cover with plastic wrap and let it rise at room temperature for 30 minutes.

Preheat oven to 350°. Bake bread 35 minutes, covering the top with aluminum foil for the last 10 minutes. Let the bread cool inside the pan for 15 minutes. Then transfer to a cooling rack to cool completely.

Combine glaze ingredients. When bread is cooled, drizzle with glaze.

2 Ingredient Dough

1   cup + 2 Tbsp. self-rising flour*
1   cup plain Greek yogurt (non-fat or regular)

By hand: Mix ingredients in a bowl and knead with a small amount of additional flour for 3-5 minutes, until smooth dough forms.

Stand Mixer: Place ingredients in a stand mixer bowl with the dough hook attachment. Mix on low speed until combined. Knead on medium speed for about 3 minutes, until a ball forms.

Turn out onto a floured surface. Sprinkle with flour. Knead a couple of times and form into a ball.

*Self-rising flour: 1 cup flour, ½ tsp. salt, 1½ tsp. baking powder. Mix.

2 Ingredient Dough Cinnamon Rolls

1   batch 2 ingredient dough
2-3 Tbsp. butter or margarine
¼   cup brown sugar
1   Tbsp. cinnamon (or to taste)
¼-½ cup vanilla icing

Preheat oven to 375°. Roll dough into a rectangle. Spread with butter. Sprinkle with brown sugar and cinnamon. Roll up dough jelly roll style. Cut into 12 pieces. Bake 18 minutes, until golden brown on top. Drizzle with vanilla icing.

2 Ingredient Dough Pizza

1   batch 2 ingredient dough (p. 102)
¾   cup pizza sauce
1¼   cups shredded Italian cheeses
     pepperoni
1   tsp. oregano

Preheat oven to 425°. Roll dough out into a large circle on a floured surface. Move the dough over to a greased baking sheet or pizza stone. Reshape dough to fill the pan.

Top with pizza sauce, shredded cheese, pepperoni and oregano.
Bake 17-20 minutes, until crust is golden brown and cheese is melted.

I ate salad for dinner!
OK... it WAS mostly croutons and tomatoes.
Really just one big crouton covered in tomato sauce and cheese.
Fine... it was pizza. I ate a pizza.

2 Ingredient Dough Pretzel Bites

1   batch 2 ingredient dough (p. 102)
½   cup boiling water
1   Tbsp. baking soda
¼   cup butter or margarine, melted
1   Tbsp. pretzel salt or coarse salt

Preheat oven to 425°. Cut the dough into four pieces. Roll each piece of dough into a long rope. Cut the ropes into small segments.

Dissolve baking soda in boiling water. Dip the dough segments into the baking soda mixture and place on a greased baking sheet.

Bake 7-10 minutes, until golden brown. Brush with melted butter and sprinkle with pretzel salt.

2 Ingredient Dough Breadsticks

1   batch 2 ingredient dough (p. 102)
2   Tbsp. butter or margarine, melted
½   tsp. garlic salt

Preheat oven to 425°. Cut the dough into six pieces. Roll each piece into a long breadstick shape and place on a greased baking sheet. Bake 10-14 minutes, until golden brown.

Mix together melted butter and garlic salt. Brush on the breadsticks.

2 Ingredient Dough Bagels

1   batch 2 ingredient dough (p. 102)
1   egg white, beaten
     coarse salt

Preheat oven to 475°. Cut the dough into six pieces. Roll each piece into a long rope and then form a circle with the dough rope, pinching the ends together where they meet. Place on a greased baking sheet.

Brush with beaten egg white and sprinkle with coarse salt. Bake 12-14 minutes, until golden brown.

Variations

- Sprinkle with cinnamon and sugar

- Sprinkle with Everything Bagel Seasoning (p. 350)

- Sprinkle with garlic and herb seasoning

2 Ingredient Dough Garlic Cheddar Rolls

1   batch 2 ingredient dough (p. 102)
½   cup Cheddar cheese, shredded
2   Tbsp. butter or margarine, melted
¼   tsp. garlic powder

Preheat oven to 475°. Flatten dough ball slightly and pour the shredded cheese into the center. Knead cheese into the dough.

Divide dough into eight pieces and roll into balls. Place on a greased baking sheet. Bake 10-14 minutes, until golden brown. Mix melted butter and garlic powder. Brush over garlic Cheddar rolls.

2 Ingredient Dough Naan Flatbread

1   batch 2 ingredient dough (p. 102)
2   Tbsp. olive oil
2   Tbsp. butter or margarine, melted (optional)
2   tsp. sea salt (optional)
1   Tbsp. cilantro, chopped (optional)

Cut dough into eight pieces. Put one piece of dough on a well floured surface and sprinkle with flour. Roll the piece of dough into a thin circle and set aside. Repeat with the remaining pieces of dough.

Warm a cast iron or non-stick skillet over medium-high heat. Brush the skillet with olive oil and then carefully add a thin circle of dough. Cook for a few minutes until it puffs up and gets brown spots. Flip and cook on the other side. Repeat with remaining dough.

Brush with melted butter and sprinkle with sea salt and cilantro, if desired.

Eggs are fantastic for your diet.
If you don't like the taste, just add cocoa, flour, sugar, butter and baking powder and bake at 350° for 20 minutes.

Buttermilk Biscuits

2	cups all-purpose flour*
1	Tbsp. baking powder
2-3	tsp. sugar (optional, to taste)
1	tsp. salt
½	cup butter flavored shortening or unsalted butter, cold
¾	cups buttermilk, cold

Preheat oven to 475° and line a baking sheet with parchment paper.

Place flour, baking powder, sugar and salt in a large mixing bowl. Whisk together until combined. Cut in shortening or butter until the pieces are no bigger than the size of a pea. Stir in buttermilk until a loose dough forms.

Knead dough with your hands a few times to gather the dough into a ball and incorporate any flour that may be left in the bottom of the bowl. Dust work surface with flour and flatten dough to a thickness of ¾ inch.

Dip a 2-inch diameter cutter into flour and cut rounds.

Place the rounds on the prepared baking sheet (with their sides barely touching). Bake 8 to 12 minutes or until golden.

Popeye's® Biscuits Copycat

½	cup butter, melted
4	cups baking mix (Bisquick)
¾	cup club soda
1	cup sour cream

Preheat oven to 400°. Melt butter in a 9x13 inch pan. Combine baking mix, club soda and sour cream. Knead lightly. Roll out dough on a floured surface and pat until about 2 inches thick. Cut with a biscuit cutter. Place in pan and turn over to coat with melted butter in the pan. Bake until golden brown.

Angel Biscuits

1   Tbsp. or 1 pkg. yeast
2   cups warm water (110°)
5   cups all purpose flour
¼   cup sugar
1   tsp. baking powder
1   tsp. baking soda
1   tsp. salt
½   cup shortening
2   cups buttermilk
     butter, cold

Preheat oven to 450°. In a measuring cup, dissolve yeast in warm water.

In a large bowl, add flour, sugar, baking powder, baking soda and salt. Cut in shortening until it resembles coarse meal.

Add yeast mixture and buttermilk. Stir just until moist. Chill 1 hour.

Knead dough on a heavily floured surface. Roll to 2 inches thick. Cut with a lightly floured biscuit cutter or a floured glass.

Place on a greased baking sheet. Rub cold butter over the tops. Bake 13 minutes, until golden.

I need to start eating healthy, but first let me eat all the junk food in the house so it doesn't tempt me.

1 Banana Bread
14 Variations

1½   cups sugar
½   cup shortening
2   eggs, beaten
1   tsp. vanilla
¼   cup sour milk
2   cups all purpose flour
½   cup raisins (optional)
1   tsp. baking powder
½   tsp. baking soda
½   tsp. salt
1   cup bananas (2 medium bananas), mashed
½ -1 cup nuts, chopped (optional)

Preheat oven to 350°. Mix all the ingredients until smooth. Pour into a greased and floured loaf pan. Bake 50-60 minutes. Makes 1 loaf.

Variations

- **Chocolate Chip Banana Bread** - Add ¾ cup semi-sweet chocolate chips to batter.

- **Coconut Banana Bread** - Add ½ cup shredded coconut to batter. Top with 2 Tbsp. shredded coconut. After baking, glaze with ½ cup powdered sugar and 4 tsp. lemon juice mixed together.

- **Chocolate Banana Bread** - Replace ½ cup flour with ½ cup baking cocoa. Bake as usual.

- **Double Chocolate Banana Bread** - Replace ½ cup flour with ½ cup baking cocoa. Add ¾ cup semi-sweet chocolate chips. Bake as usual.

- **Triple Chocolate Banana Bread** - Replace ½ cup flour with ½ cup baking cocoa. Add ¾ cup semi-sweet chocolate chips. Top with chocolate glaze. Bake as usual.

- **Chocolate Glaze** - Mix 3 Tbsp. cocoa, 2 Tbsp. melted butter, 1 cup powdered sugar, 3 Tbsp. warm water, ½ tsp. vanilla.

- **Butterscotch Banana Bread** - Add ¾ cup butterscotch chips to batter. Bake as usual.

- **Cinnamon Swirl** - Mix 2 Tbsp. butter, melted, ⅓ cup brown sugar and 2 Tbsp. cinnamon. Pour ¼ banana bread batter into a pan. Then sprinkle ¼ Cinnamon Swirl mix on top. Continue to layer in alternating layers. After all the layers are in the pan, gently swirl the banana bread batter with a spoon. Then bake as usual.

- **Blueberry Banana Bread** - Add ½ cup blueberries to the batter. Bake as usual.

- **Chocolate Raspberry Banana Bread** - Add ¾ cup semi-sweet chocolate chips, ⅓ cup raspberries and ⅓ cup chopped almonds to the batter. Bake as usual.

- **Pineapple Banana Bread** - Reduce bananas in basic recipe to ½ cup. Add ⅓ cup drained crushed pineapple and ½ cup shredded coconut. Mix into batter and bake as usual.

- **Cream Cheese Banana Bread** - Mix 8-10 oz. softened cream cheese, ⅓ cup sugar, 1 egg and 1 Tbsp. all purpose flour. Pour half of banana bread batter into greased pan. Add this cream cheese filling as the next layer. Place remaining batter on top of cream cheese filling. Bake as usual.

- **Chocolate Oatmeal Banana Bread** - Replace 1 cup of flour with 1 cup old fashioned oats. Add ¾ cup semi-sweet chocolate chips. Bake as usual.

- **Strawberry Banana Bread** - Toss 1⅓ cups fresh strawberries in 1 Tbsp. flour. Add strawberries to batter and bake as usual.

Easy Pull Apart Bread

½   cup sugar
1   tsp. cinnamon
2   (16.3 oz.) cans Grands biscuits (8 biscuits each)
1   cup brown sugar, packed
¾   cup butter or margarine, melted

Preheat oven to 325°. Lightly grease a 12 cup bundt cake pan. Mix sugar and cinnamon in a plastic bag. Separate dough into a total of 16 biscuits. Cut each biscuit into quarters. Shake in cinnamon and sugar bag to coat. Place evenly distributed in pan. Mix brown sugar and butter. Pour over biscuit pieces.

Bake 35-40 minutes or until golden brown and a toothpick inserted in the center comes out clean. Cool in pan 10 minutes. Turn upside down onto serving plate Pull apart to serve. Serve warm.

Spicy Coffee Cake

1   (15 oz.) spice cake mix
4   eggs
1   (3.4 oz.) pkg. vanilla pudding
1   cup sour cream
½   cup oil

Mix. Pour into a greased 9x13 inch pan.

Topping

2   Tbsp. butter or margarine, softened
1-2   tsp. cinnamon
¾   cup brown sugar, packed

Preheat oven to 350°. Mix topping ingredients and sprinkle on batter. Bake 30-40 minutes or until a toothpick inserted in the center comes out clean.

Sour Cream Coffee Cake

Cake

½   cup butter or margarine
1   cup sugar
2   eggs
1   cup sour cream
1   tsp. vanilla
2   cups all purpose flour
1   tsp. baking powder
1   tsp. baking soda
¼   tsp. salt

Topping

⅓   cup brown sugar, packed
¼   cup sugar
2   tsp. cinnamon
½   cup walnuts, chopped

Preheat oven to 325°. Cream butter and sugar in a bowl. Add eggs, sour cream and vanilla. Mix well. Add dry ingredients and beat until mixed. Pour into a 9x13 inch pan. Sprinkle topping on top of cake.

Bake 40 minutes.

All I ask is, if I am ever murdered,
that you would make the
chalk outline of my body 4 sizes smaller.

English Scones

(Serve with Clotted Cream (p. 326) and jam.)

2	cups all purpose flour
½	cup sugar
½	tsp. salt
2½	tsp. baking powder
½	cup butter, frozen
½	cup heavy cream or buttermilk (plus 2 Tbsp. for brushing)
1	large egg
1½	tsp. vanilla
1-1½	cups add-ins (chocolate chips, berries, nuts, fruit, etc.)

Whisk flour, sugar, salt, and baking powder together in a large bowl. Grate frozen butter. Add to flour mixture and combine with your fingers until the mixture comes together in pea-sized crumbs.

Whisk ½ cup heavy cream, egg and vanilla in a small bowl. Drizzle over flour mixture. Add desired add-ins. Mix together until everything appears moistened.

For triangle scones: Pour onto the counter and, with floured hands, work dough into a ball as best you can. Dough will be sticky. If it is too sticky, add a little more flour. If it seems too dry, add 1-2 more tablespoons of heavy cream. Press into an 8-inch disc and, with a sharp knife or bench scraper, cut into 8 wedges.

For drop scones: Drop about ¼ cup of dough each, 3 inches apart on a lined baking sheet. Brush scones with remaining heavy cream and, for extra crunch, sprinkle with coarse sugar. Place scones on a lined baking sheet and refrigerate for at least 15 minutes.

Preheat oven to 400°. Bake for 18-26 minutes or until golden brown around the edges and lightly browned on top. Larger scones take closer to 25 minutes. Remove from the oven and cool for a few minutes before topping with optional toppings listed in the ingredients.

Leftover scones keep well at room temperature for 2 days or in the refrigerator for 5 days.

Variations

- Add ½-1 teaspoon ground cinnamon
- coarse sugar, sprinkled on top
- vanilla icing
- salted caramel icing
- lemon icing
- maple icing
- brown butter icing
- lemon curd
- orange icing
- raspberry icing
- dusting of powdered sugar

My wife made coffee for me this morning and winked at me when she handed me the cup. I have never been more scared of a drink in my whole life.

Notes

Soups and Sandwiches

Soup And Sandwich Tips

- **When making any type of sandwich that will be wrapped for a while,** store your lettuce, tomato or any "wet" ingredients in a separate bag to be added later so they don't make the sandwich soggy. Add the condiments later, too. Save the extra packets of ketchup, mustard, mayonnaise and other sauces from fast food places and use them for sandwiches.

- **Do your sandwiches get smashed in lunch sacks?** Slide them into the boxes that margarine comes in. They are the perfect size.

- **Start meats and veggies in cold water.** It helps draw out the flavors.

- **Always simmer soups on the lowest temperature** you can and cover while cooking.

- **For an extra clear broth, strain through a cheesecloth.** It is not usually necessary, but if you were making broth for a special occasion, you could use this method to get it crystal clear.

- **Use dried herbs.** They work better for soups than fresh herbs.

- **Add salt to soups at the end, but other spices at the beginning.** Soup takes a lot of salt. If your soup just doesn't seem to have any flavor, chances are you need more salt.

- **If you get too much salt in your soup,** add a potato to it to cut the salty taste. (The potato will absorb some of the salt.)

- **For added zip,** add some red peppers or garlic to your soup.

- **Always add the longest cooking vegetables first,** like carrots and potatoes. Then add things that need to cook less at the end, like peas or corn.

- **Save little dabs of leftover veggies or meat** and store in the freezer. Add them to some broth and you'll have a quick free meal.

- **Ever wonder why grandma spread a thin layer of butter on her sandwiches?** The fat in the butter makes a barrier on the bread so your sandwiches don't get soggy.

Bone Broth

1-2 lbs. bones from one roasted chicken or beef, turkey or lamb
1   Tbsp. salt
1   bay leaf
1   onion
1   carrot
1   stalk celery
2   Tbsp. vinegar
     water
     parsley (optional, to taste)
     garlic (optional, to taste)

Throw everything but the optional items into a large pot. Fill to the top with water and bring it to a boil. Turn the heat down and let it simmer overnight for at least 24 hours. You can keep adding water and go up to 48 hours.

If you notice a foam on the top of your broth when it first starts cooking, just skim that off and throw it away. If desired, add parsley or garlic 30 minutes before the end of cooking.

When it is finished cooking, strain the broth to get out all of the bones and vegetables. Serve.

This broth can be used to make soups or you can use it in place of water for making rice. You can also drink it plain with some salt.

Crockpot Method

Put everything into the crockpot and cook for 24 hours on low.

Instant Pot Method

Put everything in an Instant Pot and cook on High Pressure for 3 hours. Be sure not to fill past the max capacity line.

• **You can add canned broth to your homemade broth for a stronger flavor or just for a different flavor.**

Vegetable Stock

Save vegetable scraps in the freezer. Part of the secret to having a good broth is to use a small amounts of many different veggies or equal amounts of all of the veggies. Don't think about this too much but know that having a stock with nothing but large amounts of celery and lettuce and a tiny bit of carrot will not produce the best flavored broth.

Place 4-5 cups of the vegetable scraps in a 5 quart stock pot and cover with water.

Add 1-2 bay leaves and a few peppercorns.

Bring to a boil. Turn down the heat and simmer for 45 minutes to 1 hour. Don't cook longer because the flavor will start to deteriorate after that. Strain vegetables using a colander and remove from stock.

Store the stock in containers. You can freeze it or it will last for about 5 days in the refrigerator.

This amount makes about 2 quarts of stock.

Scraps to use:

- Carrot ends
- Celery and leaves
- Squash peels
- Lettuce
- Potato
- Green beans
- Fennel
- Bell peppers
- Parsley
- Cilantro
- Mushroom stems
- Tomatoes (Remove some seeds.)

Scraps not to use:

- Cabbage
- Broccoli
- Cauliflower
- Onion skins
- Pumpkin
- Radishes
- Potatoes
- Sweet potatoes
- Turnips
- Things with strong flavor

- Root veggies like beets will turn it an awful color.
- Spoiled veggies - Wilted is ok but moldy and bad spots are not ok.

Cheeseburger Soup

¼	cup butter, divided
½	lb. ground beef
¾	cup onion, chopped
¾	cup carrots, shredded
¾	cup celery, diced
1	tsp. basil
1	tsp. dried parsley
1¾	lbs. (about 4 cups) potatoes, peeled and cubed*
3	cups chicken broth
¼	cup all purpose flour
2-3	cups Velveeta processed cheese, cubed or
	2-3 cups American Cheese slices, cut into pieces
1½	cups milk
¾	tsp. salt
¼-½	tsp. pepper
¼	cup sour cream

In a saucepan, melt 1 tablespoon butter and cook ground beef, onion, carrots, celery, basil and parsley until cooked through, about 10 minutes. Add potatoes and broth. Bring to a boil.

Reduce heat and simmer, covered, until potatoes are tender, about 10-12 minutes.

In a small pan, melt the remaining butter. Add flour. Cook and stir until bubbly, 3-5 minutes. Add to soup. Bring to a boil. Cook and stir 2 minutes.

Reduce heat to low. Stir in cheese, milk, salt and pepper. Cook until cheese melts. Remove from heat**. Blend in sour cream.

*You can use frozen cubed potatoes in place of fresh.

**To prevent soup from curdling, remove from the heat before adding sour cream.

Chicken And Rice Soup

1	Tbsp. olive oil
1	Tbsp. butter (or more oil)
1	onion, chopped
2	cloves garlic, minced or 2 tsp. minced garlic
3	carrots, cut into bite-size pieces
3	celery ribs, cut into 1 inch slices
2	vegetable or chicken bouillon cubes
½	tsp. dried parsley
½	tsp. thyme (optional)
¼	tsp. pepper, finely ground
4	cups chicken broth (If you don't have chicken broth, use 4 cups water and 4 chicken bullion cubes.)
4	cups water
1	lb. bone in, skinless chicken pieces
1	cup rice, cooked
1	Tbsp. finely chopped parsley (optional)
	salt (to taste)

Place oil and butter in a large pot over medium-high heat. Add onion and garlic. Cook for 5 minutes, until onion is translucent. Add carrots and celery. Stir for 1 minute.

Add bouillon, dried parsley, thyme (if using), pepper, chicken broth and water. Stir and add chicken. Cover with lid, simmer on medium-low for 30 minutes to an hour. Adjust heat to medium. Skim off excess foam.

Remove lid. Add rice. Stir, cover and simmer 5 minutes. Remove soup from stove.

Remove chicken into a large bowl. Shred with 2 forks. Discard bones. Then stir chicken into soup.

Stir in half the parsley. Taste for salt and add if required. Garnish with extra parsley. Serve.

Bacon Potato Soup

6   Tbsp. bacon grease
1½   cups onion, diced
12   slices bacon, fried crispy and crumbled
4   heaping cups of potatoes, diced and cooked*
2   cups water
2   cans cream of chicken soup
4   cups milk
2   tsp. salt
4   Tbsp. parsley flakes

Brown onion in bacon grease in a large pan. Add the rest of the
ingredients and heat through. Do not boil.

*This is a great way to use leftover roasted potatoes.

Busy Day Soup

1   lb. ground beef
5   cups water
1   pkg. onion soup mix
1   (28 oz.) can diced tomatoes
1   cup macaroni, uncooked
1¾   cups mixed frozen vegetables   *dehy drated*

In a large soup pot, brown ground beef. Drain fat. Pour in water, onion
soup mix and tomatoes with juice. Simmer 1 hour on medium-low.

Add macaroni and frozen vegetables. Cook 15 minutes longer on medium
heat. Serve hot.

• **For a creamy soup, add some mashed or instant potatoes.**

Minestrone

4	Tbsp. olive oil
1	medium onion, chopped
2	medium carrots, peeled and chopped
2	medium ribs celery, chopped
¼	cup tomato paste
2	cups seasonal vegetables, chopped (potatoes, yellow squash, zucchini, butternut squash, green beans or peas)
4	cloves garlic, minced or 4 tsp. minced garlic
½	tsp. dried oregano
½	tsp. thyme
1	(28 oz.) large can diced tomatoes, with their liquid or 2 (15 oz.) cans diced tomatoes
4	cups (32 oz.) chicken broth
2	cups water
1	tsp. salt
2	bay leaves
	pinch of red pepper flakes
	pepper
1	cup elbow or small shell pasta
1	(15 oz.) can Great Northern beans
2	cups baby spinach
2	tsp. lemon juice
	grated Parmesan cheese (for garnishing, optional)

Heat oil in a Dutch oven or stock pot over medium heat. Add onion, carrots and celery. Cook until softened.

Add the rest of the ingredients, except lemon juice and Parmesan cheese. Cook, covered, until pasta is al dente. Stir occasionally. Remove from heat. Remove bay leaves.

Ladle into bowls. Add a drizzle of olive oil and lemon juice. Sprinkle with Parmesan cheese.

Broccoli Cheese Soup

1	Tbsp. butter
½	medium onion, chopped
¼	cup butter
¼	cup all purpose flour
2	cups chicken stock
½	lb. fresh or frozen broccoli, chopped into bite-size pieces
1	cup carrots, sliced thin
2	cups half and half
	salt (to taste)
	pepper (to taste)
1	tsp. garlic powder (optional)
8	oz. sharp Cheddar cheese, grated
¼	tsp. nutmeg

In a stock pot, add 1 tablespoon butter and onion. Sauté.

Over medium heat, add ¼ cup butter and the flour. Stir, using a whisk, for 3-5 minutes.

Add chicken stock, broccoli and carrots and simmer for 20 minutes.

Add half and half. Season to taste with salt and pepper. Add garlic powder, if desired. If you prefer it smoother, puree to desired consistency. Return to heat and add cheese, until melted. Stir in nutmeg and serve.

I hate it when I eat the last bite
but didn't notice it was the last bite
so I didn't have a chance to mentally
prepare myself for closure.

Panera® Black Bean Soup Copycat

1	onion, finely chopped
2	cloves garlic, minced or 2 tsp. minced garlic
2	stalks celery, finely chopped
¼	large bell pepper, finely chopped
2	small chicken or vegetable bouillon cubes
1-1½ cups water	
2	(15 oz.) cans black beans, undrained
½	tsp. salt
½	tsp. cumin
½	lemon or lime, juiced
1½	Tbsp. cornstarch, mixed with 1½ Tbsp. water

Toppings (optional)

Cheddar cheese, shredded
avocado, diced
tortilla chips, crushed
sour cream

Combine onion, garlic, celery, bell pepper, bouillon, and water in a pot and simmer 10 minutes.

Add half a can of beans, salt, and cumin. Cook 5 minutes.

Puree soup with an immersion blender directly in the pot or in batches in a regular blender. Then pour back into the pot.

Add remaining black beans, lemon or lime juice and cornstarch to the soup and simmer until thickened.

Easy Chili

1	lb. ground beef
½	onion, diced
1	tsp. pepper
½	tsp. garlic salt
2½	cups tomato sauce
1	cup salsa
4	Tbsp. chili seasoning mix (p.338)
1	(15 oz.) can light red kidney beans
1	(15 oz.) can dark red kidney beans

In a large saucepan over medium heat, combine the ground beef and the onion. Sauté 10 minutes or until the meat is browned and the onion is tender. Drain grease, if desired.

Add the rest of the ingredients. Reduce heat to low and simmer for at least an hour.

- **You can use 1 bouillon cube in place of 1 teaspoon of bouillon granules. You might also find it useful to know that one cube or teaspoon of granules dissolved in a cup of hot water is equal to 1 cup of broth.**

- **When you have just a few veggies left from roasted veggies, don't toss them. Chop them up and use them in your favorite casserole, chili or meatloaf recipes. The roasted taste of the veggies adds more flavor to ordinary recipes.**

- **To bulk up any soup, add rice, pasta, potatoes, barley or beans. This really helps to stretch the soup if you have unexpected company coming.**

The Best White Chili

Tawra's recipe was a 1st place chili cookoff winner.

1	Tbsp. olive oil
1	lb. boneless, skinless chicken breast halves, cut into ½ inch cubes
1	onion, chopped
2	cloves garlic, minced or 2 tsp. minced garlic
2	(15.5 oz.) cans great Northern beans, rinsed and drained
1	(14.5 oz.) can chicken broth
2	(4 oz.) cans chopped green chilies
1	tsp. salt
1	tsp. cumin
1	tsp. oregano
½	tsp. pepper
¼	tsp. cayenne pepper
¼	cup cornstarch
2	Tbsp. butter
1	cup sour cream
½	cup heavy whipping cream

Heat the oil in a large saucepan. Sauté the chicken, onion and garlic until the chicken is cooked through.

Mix the great Northern beans, chicken broth, green chilies, salt, cumin, oregano, pepper and cayenne pepper into the chicken mixture. Bring it to a boil.

Reduce the heat and simmer until the flavors have blended, about 30 minutes.

Mix the cornstarch with about ¼ cup of water. Put it in the pan and bring it to a boil until the chili is thickened.

Remove from the heat and add butter, sour cream and whipping cream.

Clam Chowder

½	cup butter
1½	large onions, chopped
¾	cup all purpose flour
1	qt. shucked clams, with liquid
6	(8 oz.) jars clam juice
1	lb. boiled potatoes, peeled and chopped
3	cups half and half
	salt and pepper (to taste)
¼	tsp. dried dill

Melt butter in a large pot over medium heat. Add onions and sauté until clear. Stir in flour and cook on low heat 2-4 minutes, stirring frequently. Set aside to cool.

In a separate pot, bring clams and clam juice to a boil. Reduce heat and simmer 15 minutes.

In a small saucepan, cover peeled potatoes with water. Bring to a boil and cook until potatoes are tender, about 15 minutes. Drain and set aside.

Slowly pour hot clam stock into butter/flour mixture, while stirring constantly. Continue stirring and slowly bring to a boil. Reduce heat and add cooked potatoes. Mix in half and half, salt and pepper and dill. Heat through but do not boil.

Want a good soup recipe?
Just let your ice cream melt.

Corn Chowder

1	Tbsp. butter
1	medium onion, chopped
2	medium potatoes, peeled and diced
1	bag frozen corn
4	cups chicken broth
2	tomatoes, cored, seeded and chopped (optional)
	or 1 can diced tomatoes
1	cup milk
	salt and pepper (to taste)
½	cup parsley, chopped (optional)

Melt butter in a saucepan over medium-high heat. Add onion and potatoes. Cook, stirring occasionally, until onion softens, about 5 minutes. Add corn, chicken broth and tomatoes. Cook, stirring, for another minute or two.

Bring to a boil, then lower heat to a simmer.

When potatoes are tender, add milk and heat through. Salt and pepper, to taste. Garnish with the parsley, and serve.

When I was little, I didn't care about things like what to wear.
My parents dressed me.
Looking at some of my old pictures,
it is obvious that
my parents didn't care either.

Hungarian Goulash

2   Tbsp. butter
2   medium onions, diced
1   tsp. caraway seeds (optional)
2   Tbsp. paprika
1½   lb. stewing beef, trimmed and cut into 1 inch cubes
¼   cup all purpose flour
2   cups beef broth or water
1   cup canned diced tomatoes
3   cups potatoes (optional)
1½   cups carrots (optional)
1   tsp. salt
¼   tsp. pepper

In a large pot, melt butter and add onions. Cook till translucent. Stir in caraway seeds (if using) and paprika.

In a bowl, dredge the stew beef with flour. Add beef to the onion mixture and cook about 2-3 minutes.

Slowly add about ¼ cup of the beef broth to lift the brown bits off the bottom of the pan. Then add remaining broth, diced tomatoes, potatoes and carrots (if using) and salt and pepper. Stir and bring to a boil. Cover and reduce to a simmer for about 1½-2 hours or until beef is tender.

- **Use kitchen shears to cut green onions and chives. It is much faster and safer.**

How To Make A Soggy Free Sandwich

This is the way to make a sandwich so the bread does not become soggy.

bread
meat
tomato
mayonnaise
mustard
catsup
lettuce
cheese

Place two slices of bread on a counter. Place sandwich ingredients you would like in the order listed on 1 piece of bread (so the wettest ingredients are in the middle of the other ingredients). Place second piece of bread on top. When the condiments and tomatoes are on the inside of the sandwich, your sandwich won't become soggy.

Soggy Free Peanut Butter & Jelly Sandwich

bread
peanut butter
jelly

Place bread on counter. Spread a thin amount of peanut butter on EACH slice of bread. Place one tablespoon jelly on one slice on the peanut butter. Then put the other slice of bread on top. The fat in the peanut butter keeps the bread from getting soggy from the jelly.

Grilled Cheese Sandwiches

2 slices American cheese*
2 slices white bread
  mayonnaise**, butter or margarine

Spread one side of bread with mayonnaise, butter or margarine. Place in a pan on medium heat. Add cheese. Spread second piece of bread with mayonnaise, butter or margarine. Place on top of the cheese, with the butter side up. When bottom is golden brown, flip and cook until second side is golden brown.

*You can use any kind of cheese.

**Mayonnaise adds a great flavor. It also reduces the chance of burning your grilled cheese as easily as with butter.

Variations

Ham and Cheese: Add 1 slice ham in between the cheeses.

Bacon and Tomato: Add 3 slices bacon and 1 slice tomato between the cheese.

Triple Cheese: 1 slice each Cheddar, muenster and Swiss cheese

Green Chile: Spread drained green chiles between cheese.

Bacon: Add bacon between cheese.

Apple: Add sliced apples between cheese.

Spicy Nacho: 1 slice Monterrey Jack or American cheese, pickled jalapeño slices and 1 slice Cheddar

Grilled Cheese Fingers: Cut off the crusts and cut the sandwich into strips.

Spicy: 1 Tbsp. mayonnaise with ¼ tsp. Sriracha. Make grilled cheese, replacing mayonnaise with the spicy mayonnaise mixture.

Cheddar and Pickles: White Cheddar and sliced pickles between the cheese.

Garlic Ham and Cheese: 2 slices Monterey Jack and 1 slice ham. Lightly sprinkle garlic powder on top of the cheese.

Pesto: Place 1 slice provolone on 1 slice white bread. Spread pesto on cheese. Top with 1 slice mozzarella. Top with another slice of bread.

Avocado: Toss ¼ sliced avocado with lime juice, to taste. Place between 2 slices pepper jack cheese and grill.

Swiss Mushroom: Spread 2 slices rye bread with Thousand Island dressing. Use 2 slices Swiss cheese. Place sautéed mushrooms and onions in between cheese and grill.

Bagel Grilled Cheese: Spread bagel with mayonnaise and spicy mustard, 2 slices muenster and 2 slices salami and grill.

Cajun: Use 2 slices provolone. Stir a pinch of Cajun seasoning into mayonnaise and grill.

Blue Cheese and Onion: 2 slices marbled rye bread, 2 slices muenster, soft blue cheese and caramelized onions

Pizza: 2 slices provolone with pepperoni and spaghetti sauce in between.

Baked Ham And Cheese Sandwiches

12   slices bread
3   Tbsp. butter or margarine, softened
3   Tbsp. Dijon mustard
6   slices ham
12   slices Cheddar or Swiss cheese
1   medium tomato, thinly sliced
4   eggs
¼   cup milk
¼   tsp. pepper

Butter one side of 6 slices of the bread. Lay the bread, butter side down, in a greased 9x13 inch pan. Spread mustard on top of the bread. Layer the ham, cheese and tomato on top of the mustard. Top each sandwich with another slice of bread. Butter the outsides of the top pieces of bread. Cut each sandwich in half.

Beat the eggs, milk and pepper. Pour over the sandwiches. Cover and refrigerate overnight. Remove from the refrigerator 30 minutes before baking. Preheat oven to 375° and bake, uncovered, for 30 minutes or until the bread is golden brown and the cheese is melted.

I'm glad I don't have to hunt for my food.
I don't even know where sandwiches live.

Italian French Dip Sandwiches

Dipping Sauce

1   (8 oz.) can tomato sauce
¼   tsp. basil
¼   tsp. crushed red pepper flakes
⅛   tsp. garlic powder

Combine and simmer about 15 minutes.

Sandwiches

1   lb. bulk (ground) Italian or country sausage
1   med. onion, thinly sliced and separated
8   slices mozzarella or provolone cheese
8   slices French bread
     butter or margarine*

Shape the sausage into patties and fry. Remove from the pan and sauté the onions in the sausage drippings.

Place a slice of cheese on each of 4 pieces of bread. Top with the patties, onions and another slice of cheese each. Then place another piece of bread on top of each one.

Spread the outside of the bread with butter or margarine and cook until golden brown. Serve and dip in dipping sauce.

To save money, you can use less meat, make smaller patties and use only 1 slice of cheese for each sandwich.

*If using butter, make sure to cook it on low so it doesn't burn.

Cheesy French Dip

    garlic butter
    sandwich buns
    Cheddar cheese, grated
1   roast, slow cooked

Make some garlic butter, either by sautéing a little garlic in some butter or sprinkling some garlic powder (to taste) into some soft butter.

Spread each side of a bun with the garlic butter and sprinkle with grated cheese. Broil until the cheese is melted. Lay thin slices of roast on one bun and top with the other. Serve some of the roast broth on the side to dip the sandwiches in.

Pizza Hoagies

½-1 lb. ground beef or Italian sausage, cooked or pepperoni
1   jar pizza or spaghetti sauce
8   oz. mozzarella cheese, grated
    Hoagie buns (or hot dog buns)

Place a couple of tablespoons each of all of the above into a hoagie bun. You can adjust the amounts to how much you want in each bun. If desired, wrap in foil and bake in the oven at 350° for about 15 minutes.

Freezer Option

Wrap sandwiches individually in foil and freeze. Reheat in foil in oven at 350° for 25-30 minutes or microwave for about a minute. The time will vary depending on your microwave.

Philly Cheesesteak

	olive oil
1	white onion, thinly sliced
1	green bell pepper, thinly sliced (optional)
2	tsp. garlic, minced
	salt (to taste)
	pepper (to taste)
½	lb. deli roast beef, thinly sliced
½	lb. provolone cheese, thinly sliced
1	loaf Italian bread or French bread or 2 large hoagie or sub rolls
	marinara sauce (for topping, optional)

In a large sauté pan, heat a small amount of olive oil over medium-high heat. Add the onion and bell pepper. Cook, stirring, until caramelized. Add the garlic, salt and pepper and cook for about 30 seconds. Push the mixture off to one side of the pan. Add the meat to the hot part of the pan.

Cook, continuously flipping the meat over and slightly chopping the meat into slightly smaller pieces, which should take about 2 minutes.

Mix the meat, caramelized onions and bell pepper together.

Divide into 2 portions, and top both portions with the cheese to melt.

If using Italian or French bread, cut the bread in half, crosswise, and slice lengthwise to open for the 2 sandwiches.

Hollow out some of the soft white bread part from inside. Place face down on top of the meat and cheese.

When the cheese is melted, flip the sandwiches over and add topping, if desired, and serve immediately.

Meatball Sub

12   small meatballs, pre-cooked
2   cups marinara sauce
4   sub sandwich rolls
       butter
       garlic powder
1   cup Italian cheese, shredded

Warm meatballs in marinara sauce. Cut rolls in half, leaving the halves attached. Spread butter on the inside of each half of each roll. Sprinkle garlic on each half. Place 3 meatballs with sauce on each roll. Top with ¼ cup cheese on each sub.

Place under broiler to melt cheese, if desired.

Freezer Option

Wrap sandwiches individually in foil and freeze. Reheat in foil in oven at 350° for 25-30 minutes.

Reuben Sandwich

4   slices rye bread
3-4   Tbsp. butter, softened
¼   cup Thousand Island dressing
4   slices Swiss cheese
½   lb. cooked corned beef, warmed
½   cup sauerkraut, drained

Butter one side of each slice of bread. On the other side of each slice spread Thousand Island dressing. Lay 2 slices of bread into pan with butter side down and layer with cheese, corned beef, sauerkraut and a second slice of cheese. Top with another slice of bread butter side out.

Turn on to medium heat and cover with lid. Cook until cheese is melted and bread is golden brown. Flip and cook on the other side.

Monte Cristo

2   eggs
       salt and pepper (to taste)
4   slices sturdy white bread (or your preference of white bread)
2   Tbsp. yellow mustard
2   Tbsp. mayonnaise
½   lb. thick sliced baked ham
½   oz. Gruyère cheese, shredded
2   Tbsp. butter

Beat eggs in a shallow dish (large enough to fit a sandwich) along with a few pinches of salt and pepper. Set aside.

Assemble sandwiches, adding mustard, mayonnaise, ham, cheese, salt and pepper to the bread, as desired. Slightly compress sandwich.

Heat skillet over medium heat. Add butter and allow to melt.

Dip and coat each sandwich in beaten egg. Then place in skillet. Cook sandwiches 2-3 minutes on each side, until browned and cheese has melted.

> If you are wondering about my cooking skills, I have been asked to bring paper towels to our family gathering.

British Cucumber Sandwiches

8   slices soft white bread, with crusts cut off*
     butter, softened
     cucumber**

Spread butter on two pieces of bread. Peel cucumbers and slice thinly. Lay on buttered bread. Place second piece of bread on top. Slice into triangles or fingers. Serve with tea.

*Save crusts for bread crumbs or croutons.

**You can make radish sandwiches by thinly slicing radishes instead of cucumbers.

American Cucumber Sandwiches

1   cucumber, thinly sliced
1   (8 oz.) pkg. cream cheese, softened
¼   cup mayonnaise
¼   tsp. onion powder
¼   tsp. garlic powder
8   slices soft white bread, with crusts cut off*

Place sliced cucumbers between paper towels to remove moisture. Mix remaining ingredients, except bread. Spread one side of each bread slice with cream cheese mix. Layer one slice of bread with cucumber slices and top with another slice. Cut into triangles.

*Save crusts for bread crumbs or croutons.

Southwestern Veggie Wraps

You can easily add some cooked ground beef
or chopped chicken to these wraps if you like.

1	small onion, chopped
1	clove garlic, minced
1	Tbsp. vegetable oil
1	(15 oz.) can black beans, rinsed and drained
1½	cups fresh or frozen corn, thawed
1	medium red bell pepper, chopped
1	cup zucchini, chopped
	jalapeno (optional, to taste)
⅔	cup water
1	tsp. chili powder
½	tsp. dried oregano
½	tsp. cumin
	salt and pepper (to taste)
1	Tbsp. cornstarch
2	Tbsp. water
	tortillas
	salsa
	sour cream

In a large skillet, sauté onion and garlic in oil.

Add veggies, water and spices. (Don't add the cornstarch yet.) Bring to a boil. Reduce heat and simmer, uncovered, for about 10-15 minutes, until most of the liquid is gone.

Combine cornstarch with 2 tablespoons water. Stir into veggie mixture and bring back to a boil until thickened, about 1 minute. Spoon ⅔ cup of the mixture onto each tortilla. Top with salsa and sour cream.

Cobb Salad Wraps

Even though this recipe has a lot of ingredients, it is really easy and you can do some of the prep work ahead of time.

Dressing

2   Tbsp. lemon juice
1½   tsp. Dijon mustard
1   clove garlic, minced
¼   tsp. salt
⅛   tsp. pepper
1   Tbsp. olive oil or vegetable oil

Mix ingredients in a bowl and whisk well.

Filling

1½   cups chicken, cooked and shredded
1   avocado, chopped
4   bacon slices, cooked and crumbled
1   green onion, sliced
2   Tbsp. chopped ripe olives
2   Tbsp. blue cheese, crumbled

Toss the above ingredients into the dressing. Then layer the following.

Wrap

4   lettuce leaves
4   (8 inch) flour tortillas, warmed
1   medium tomato, chopped

Lay one lettuce leaf on each tortilla. Top with the chicken mixture, dividing the mixture evenly between the 4 tortillas. Sprinkle with tomatoes. Roll and close with a toothpick.

Notes

Sides

Vegetable Tips

- **If you can't use all of your zucchini right away**, shred it and then steam it for 1-2 minutes, until it is translucent. Drain and put it in measured portions in freezer containers. Use in breads or muffins.

- **Sugar can add flavor without sweetness**. Add a little of it to your veggies like mashed potatoes, tomatoes, squash or carrots. Sugar can really enhance their flavor. Not much, just a couple of teaspoons, and you don't taste the sugar.

- **Leftover mashed potatoes?** Place leftover mashed potatoes in a greased muffin tin. Top with chopped onions, crumbled bacon or cooked sausage, Parmesan cheese and a dab of butter. Bake at 400° for 15-20 minutes. Serve warm.

- **For extra special mashed potatoes**, add some grated Cheddar cheese, French fried onion rings and crumbled bacon or bacon bits. Beat until smooth.

- **Leftover baked potatoes** are good for breakfast. Cube potatoes and fry in bacon grease.

- **Slice leftover baked potatoes into quarters.** Roll in melted butter and Parmesan cheese. Bake at 350° for about 20 minutes.

- **Stir about 1 teaspoon of bacon grease** into your green beans while you are heating them. Add a small amount of onion salt and you have green beans that are big on flavor with very little work.

- **For a different variation on corn on the cob,** cook it like you normally do. Then, after you have buttered it, sprinkle with Parmesan cheese and garlic powder.

- **If you have an extra package of the cheese** that comes in a box of macaroni and cheese dinner, sprinkle some of it on a piece of buttered corn for another tasty variation.

How To Roast Vegetables

Heat oven to 400°. Lightly toss vegetables with oil and seasonings, as desired. Then roast vegetables according to the following times.

20 minutes or less

Asparagus
Kale
Mushrooms
Tomatoes

20-30 minutes

Broccoli
Cauliflower
Eggplant
Green beans
Green peppers
Onion
Zucchini

30 minutes or more

Beets
Butternut squash
Carrots
Potatoes
Pumpkin
Spaghetti squash
Sweet potatoes

Oven Roasted Vegetables

Any combination of vegetables will work for this recipe.
Just dump it all in and don't measure.

3	potatoes
2	peppers
2	heads broccoli or 1 bag frozen florets
4	carrots
1	onion
¼	cup oil
6	cloves garlic, minced or 2 Tbsp. minced garlic or 1 tsp. garlic powder
1	tsp. onion powder
1	tsp. paprika
1	tsp. salt

Preheat oven to 475°. Cut veggies into about 1 inch pieces and place on a baking sheet or 9x13 inch pan. Sprinkle with oil, garlic, onion powder, paprika and salt. Stir until vegetables are evenly coated. Roast 35 to 40 minutes, stirring every 10 minutes, or until vegetables are cooked through and browned.

Italian Roasted Vegetables

½	lb. mushrooms
1½	cups baby carrots
1	medium onion, cut into ½ inch thick wedges
1	large bell pepper, cut into strips
⅓	cup zesty Italian dressing
¼	cup grated Parmesan cheese

Preheat oven to 450°. Toss everything together. Spray a baking pan (about 15x10 inch) with cooking spray and spread vegetables on the pan. Bake about 25 minutes, until vegetables are tender. Sprinkle with a little more Parmesan cheese when done.

Restaurant Style Baked Potatoes

4   large baking potatoes, like russet
1   tsp. bacon grease or olive oil
     sea salt (or any large grained salt)
¼   cup butter

Preheat oven to 450°.

Clean potatoes. Rub the skin of each potato with the oil and a little salt. Pierce the skins in three or four places with a fork. Wrap in foil.

Place potatoes in the oven and roast 45 minutes to an hour, depending on the size of the potatoes, until they offer no resistance when a fork is inserted in the centers. Serve with butter and/or sour cream.

Jazzed Up Baked Potatoes

While you are baking your main dish, such as chicken, throw some potatoes in the oven to bake along with it. Wrap the potatoes in foil, put in a pan and cover with foil or, if there is room, put them in the pan with the main dish.

When you serve the potatoes, use a flavored dip like French onion dip or garlic dip instead of just putting butter or sour cream on them.

You could also flavor sour cream or yogurt with your favorite herbs and use that for the potatoes.

Twice Baked Potatoes

4	russet potatoes or large Yukon Gold potatoes
	oil or bacon grease
1½	cups cheese, shredded
½	tsp. garlic powder
¼	cup sour cream
¼	cup buttermilk
¼	cup butter, room temperature
½	onion, chopped
4	strips bacon cut into ¼" strips, cooked crisp, divided to leave a bit for topping
	salt (to taste)
	pepper (to taste)
	garnish: cheese, onion, bacon, butter, parsley, chives

Preheat oven to 400°. Rub each potato with oil or bacon grease. Sprinkle with salt. Wrap in foil and bake 45 minutes to 1 hour, until fork inserts easily. Remove the potatoes from the oven. Leave the oven on.

Cool 10 minutes. Cut the potatoes in half lengthwise. Leaving a ⅛-¼ inch thickness of flesh in each shell, carefully scoop out the potato flesh into a bowl.

Transfer potato shells onto a greased baking sheet. Bake 10 minutes. (This is so the shells can crisp a little and hold their shape after filling).

Mash potato flesh. Mix it, together with cheese, garlic powder, sour cream, buttermilk, butter, onions and bacon, until smooth. Season with salt and pepper.

Remove shells from the oven and set the oven to broil. Fill the potato shells, mounding in the middle, with the mashed potato mixture. Sprinkle tops with additional cheese, onion, bacon and butter, as desired.

Broil until the cheese has melted and the potatoes are spotty brown and a little crispy on top, about 5-10 minutes. Watch closely.

Cool 10 minutes and serve.

Cheese Herb Potatoes

8	medium potatoes
½	cup butter, melted
2	tsp. salt
½	tsp. pepper
⅔	cup Cheddar cheese, shredded
⅓	cup Parmesan cheese, shredded
2	Tbsp. each minced fresh chives, sage and thyme

Preheat oven to 425°. With a sharp knife, cut each potato crosswise into ⅛ inch slices, leaving slices attached at the bottom. Fan potatoes slightly and place in a greased 9x13 inch baking dish.

In a small bowl, mix butter, salt and pepper. Drizzle over potatoes.

Bake, uncovered, 50-55 minutes or until potatoes are tender.

In the same small bowl, toss cheeses with herbs. Sprinkle over potatoes. Bake about 5 minutes longer or until cheese is melted.

I love my kids. Not enough to turn the fish sticks over half way through cooking, but I love them.

Ranch Potatoes

If you have leftover baked potatoes or boiled potatoes, you can chop them up and use them in recipes like this one or in recipes that call for frozen hash browns.

8-10 small red potatoes, quartered
¼   cup vegetable oil
4   tsp. ranch seasoning mix

Preheat oven to 450°. Place potatoes on an ungreased baking sheet. Drizzle oil on top. Sprinkle ranch seasoning on top. Mix well, until coated. Bake 30 to 35 minutes or until potatoes are brown and crisp.

Garlic Potatoes

10-20 small red or white potatoes, quartered
¼   cup olive oil
1½   tsp. sea salt (or any large grained salt)
1   tsp. pepper
2   Tbsp. (6 cloves) garlic, minced
2   Tbsp. fresh parsley, minced

Preheat oven to 400°.

Toss potatoes in a bowl with the olive oil, salt, pepper and garlic. Toss until they are well coated. Transfer to a sheet pan and spread out into 1 layer. Roast in the oven 45 minutes to 1 hour or until browned and crisp. Flip twice during cooking in order to ensure even browning.

Remove the potatoes from the oven. Toss with parsley, season to taste and serve hot.

Acorn Squash

1   medium acorn squash, halved and seeded
1   Tbsp. butter
2   Tbsp. brown sugar

Preheat oven to 350°.

Turn acorn squash halves, flesh side down, onto a cookie sheet. Bake until they begin to soften, about 30 to 45 minutes.

Remove squash from the oven. Turn over the halves so the flesh is facing upwards. Divide butter and brown sugar and place into the squash halves. Place squash in the oven and bake another 30 minutes.

Spaghetti Squash

1   spaghetti squash, cut in half

Preheat oven to 350°.

Place spaghetti squash with cut sides down on a baking sheet. Bake 30 minutes or until a sharp knife can be inserted with only a little resistance. Remove squash from oven and set aside to cool enough to be easily handled. Use forks to scrape out squash strands. Serve with any type of pasta sauce.

• **Cook veggies with bouillon cubes instead of salt for a tastier flavor.**

Dilled Cucumbers

5-6   cucumbers, peeled and thinly sliced
1   cup sour cream
1½   tsp. salt
¼   tsp. sugar
1   tsp. dill seed
1½   tsp. parsley, chopped
2   Tbsp. lemon juice
1   Tbsp. onion, finely chopped
2   Tbsp. dill pickles, chopped
      dash of pepper

Mix everything except the cucumbers. Pour mixture over the cucumbers.

Cucumbers In Dressing

1   cup mayonnaise
¼   cup sugar
¼   cup vinegar
¼   tsp. salt
4   cups cucumbers, sliced

Mix the first 4 ingredients in a large bowl. Add the cucumbers and stir to coat. Cover and chill for 2 hours.

• **When storing fresh herbs like parsley or dill, whether they're store bought or home grown, trim about half of an inch off of the stems. Place them in a glass or jar with water as you would a vase of flowers and store in the refrigerator. This will make them last longer.**

Baked Onion Rings

2   large sweet onions
2   eggs, beaten
1½   cups corn flakes, crushed
2   tsp. sugar
1   tsp. paprika
¼   tsp. garlic salt
¼   tsp. seasoned salt

Preheat oven to 375°. Cut the onions into ½ inch slices and separate into rings. Place the eggs in a shallow dish. Mix everything else together in another dish. Dip the onion rings into the eggs first, then in the corn flake mix. Lay on a greased baking sheet. Bake 20-25 minutes, until tender.

Deluxe Stuffed Peppers

4   large green bell peppers, with tops cut off and seeded

Filling

2   cups cooked rice
1   cup Cheddar cheese, shredded
½   cup sour cream
1   (16 oz.) can Ranch Style beans, undrained
1   (11 oz.) can Mexican whole kernel corn (You can use regular
        corn seasoned with a little chili powder.)

Preheat oven to 350°. Mix filling ingredients and place ½ cup of the filling mixture into each pepper half. Then place the peppers into an ungreased 9x13 inch glass baking dish or pan. Cover with foil and bake 50-60 minutes, or until tender. Garnish with salsa. Serve with tortilla chips and extra salsa and rice.

• **If you have leftover tomato paste, place in ice cube trays or tiny containers and freeze.**

Bacon Wrapped Corn

large ears of corn, husks removed
bacon
chili powder

Wrap each ear of corn with bacon. Sprinkle with chili powder. Grill, uncovered, for 20 minutes over medium heat until the corn is tender and the bacon is cooked. Turn once.

Crockpot Cream Corn

1   (8 oz.) pkg. cream cheese
½   cup butter
4   cups or 2 (16 oz.) pkgs. frozen, fresh or canned corn
½   cup milk
1   Tbsp. sugar
     salt and pepper (to taste)

Warm cream cheese and butter until softened and mix. Place all ingredients in a crockpot and cook on high 2-4 hours or low 4-6 hours.

• **To make buttering corn easier, spread butter on a piece of bread (the heel works best). Then wrap the bread around the corn and quickly rub. Add more butter to the bread as you need it.**

Crunchy Asparagus

1½ lbs. fresh asparagus, cut into 2 inch pieces
1   cup celery, thinly sliced
2   (8 oz.) cans sliced water chestnuts, drained
¼   cup slivered almonds, toasted
2   Tbsp. soy sauce
2   Tbsp. butter or margarine

In a saucepan, cook the asparagus and celery in a small amount of water for 5-6 minutes, until crisp and tender. Drain. Add the rest of the ingredients and heat through. Serves 8-10.

Garlic Lime Asparagus

1   tsp. butter or margarine
1   Tbsp. olive oil
1   clove garlic, minced
¼   medium onion, minced
1   bunch asparagus spears, trimmed
¼   lime, squeezed (lemon juice works in a pinch)
     salt and pepper (to taste)

In a skillet, cook garlic and onion in butter and oil for 1-2 minutes. Stir in asparagus and cook until tender, about 5-10 minutes. When ready to serve, squeeze lime juice on top. Add salt and pepper.

- **When cooking, place veggies that grow underground, like potatoes, carrots, beets and turnips in cold water and then boil. Place veggies that grow above ground, like beans, peas and corn, in boiling water.**

Baked Beans Texas Style

Place the following in a 3½ quart crockpot:

1	lb. sausage, browned and drained
4	(16 oz.) cans baked beans*
1	(4 oz.) can chopped green chilies
1	small onion, chopped**
1	cup barbecue sauce
½	cup brown sugar (a little less if your beans are already sweetened)
1	Tbsp. garlic powder
1	Tbsp. chili powder
	Tabasco sauce (to taste)

Cook on high for 2 hours. Then turn down to low for 4-5 hours.

*These are very runny baked beans. If you like them thick, drain 2 of the cans of beans (or stir 2 tablespoons of cornstarch into the juice, which will thicken it).

**For extra flavor, fry the onion with the sausage or add some pieces of bacon with the other ingredients. Experiment and add a bit of mustard for a nice flavor.

- **If you have leftover chili or leftover beans from a bean dish, use them in place of hamburger for nachos the next day.**

Green Beans With Mushrooms

2   Tbsp. onion, chopped
2   tsp. bacon grease, butter or margarine
¼   cup fresh mushrooms
1   lb. fresh or frozen green beans, cooked and drained
      or one 15 oz. can green beans
      salt and pepper (to taste)

Sauté onion in bacon grease. Add mushrooms and cook 1 minute. Pour over the beans. Salt and pepper to taste.

Salsa Green Beans

1   lb. green beans, fresh, canned or frozen
1   (16 oz.) jar salsa
1   tsp. olive oil

Cook green beans until tender. Add salsa and olive oil. Simmer 5-10 minutes, until the flavors are blended.

Lemony Green Beans

¼   cup fresh mushrooms, sliced
1   Tbsp. olive or vegetable oil
1   small can green beans
      salt and pepper (to taste)
2   Tbsp. lemon juice
1   tsp. Dijon mustard

Sauté mushrooms in oil. Add green beans and heat through. Place in a serving dish. Salt and pepper to taste. Mix lemon juice and mustard and drizzle over beans.

Vegetable Stir Fry

¾   cup baby carrots, quartered lengthwise
4   cups fresh broccoli
2   tsp. vegetable oil
1   medium zucchini, halved lengthwise and sliced
½   tsp. salt
¼   tsp. pepper

In a nonstick skillet, stir fry the carrots, broccoli and oil for 5 minutes. Add everything else and stir fry 5 more minutes, or until everything is tender.

Grilled Mixed Veggies

1   medium yellow squash, peeled and sliced
1   medium zucchini, peeled and sliced
6   fresh mushrooms, sliced
2   large tomatoes, each cut into 6 pieces
1   sweet red pepper, sliced thin
1   green pepper, sliced thin
½   cup baby carrots
¼   cup ranch dressing
¼   cup Italian dressing

Mix veggies. Divide and place onto 6 squares of heavy duty foil. Mix dressings and drizzle over the veggies. Fold over each square and seal the edges well. Grill 10-13 minutes on each side.

- **Line the vegetable drawer in your refrigerator with a paper towel or press and seal. A paper towel helps to absorb the liquid from your vegetables. Then, next time you clean out the drawer, just scoop up the paper towel, crumbs and all, and toss.**

- **How about making a garden vegetable pizza with all of those garden vegetables that you haven't figured out how to use? Use zucchini, diced tomatoes, mushrooms, onions and bell peppers.**

Foolproof Brown Rice

1½ cups brown rice
2⅓ cups water
2   tsp. butter or margarine
1   tsp. salt

Preheat oven to 375°. Spread rice into an 8 inch square glass baking dish.

In a separate pan, bring water, butter and salt to a boil, keeping a close eye on it. Remove immediately after it starts boiling. Immediately pour over rice in baking dish. Cover tightly with foil. Bake on center rack in oven 1 hour. Remove from oven and fluff with a fork.

*For a quick fried rice, add cooked peas and carrots and desired amount of soy sauce.

Onion Rice

1   Tbsp. vegetable oil
1   red onion, chopped
1   cup rice
1   tsp. pepper
2   cups chicken broth

Heat the oil in a saucepan. Stir in the onion and cook until almost tender. Stir in rice. Continue cooking, making sure everything is coated with oil. When onion is tender and rice begins to brown lightly, season with pepper and add broth. Bring to a boil. Reduce heat to low. Cover and simmer
20-25 minutes.

For even more flavor, you can add half of a package of onion soup mix if you have some on hand.

Mexicorn Rice

1   cup rice
2   cups water
2   (12 oz.) cans Mexicorn, drained
1   tsp. salt
½   tsp. onion powder
¼   tsp. pepper
2   Tbsp. pimento, chopped

Cook rice in water in a 2 quart saucepan. When cooked, add remaining ingredients and mix. Serves 4-6.

Rice Patio Salad

This recipe is a nice alternative to the usual potato salad.

1   (10 oz.) pkg. frozen peas
½   tsp. salt
1½   cups water
1⅓   cups rice, cooked
1   Tbsp. onion, minced or 1 tsp. onion powder
¾   cup mayonnaise
½   cup dill pickle, chopped

In a saucepan, bring peas, salt and water to boil. Remove from heat and stir in rice and onion. Cover and let stand for 13 minutes. Cool. Add mayonnaise and pickle. Chill. Serves 6.

• **Add 1 tsp. lemon juice to the boiling water to make rice fluffier and whiter.**

Macaroni And Cheese

1½   cups dry elbow macaroni
3   Tbsp. butter
3   Tbsp. all purpose flour
2   cups milk, not skim
½   tsp. salt
½   tsp. pepper
2   cups cheese, shredded (Cheddar, Swiss)
     parsley, chopped (optional)

Preheat oven to 350°. Bring a pot of water to a boil. Add a generous sprinkling of salt and the pasta.

While the pasta cooks, melt the butter in a skillet or pot large enough to hold the pasta when it's done. Add the flour and stir over medium heat until the mixture is lightly browned, about 1-2 minutes.
Add milk and whisk to remove any lumps. Add salt and pepper. Cook over medium-high heat until mixture thickens and starts to bubble, about 6 minutes.

Stir in cheese and whisk until smooth and melted. Turn off the heat.
When the pasta is almost done, but still firm, remove from heat and drain. Stir the pasta into the sauce. Bake in a greased 2 quart dish (or 8x8 inch baking pan) for 20-25 minutes, until browned and bubbly. Sprinkle with parsley, if desired.

If you want it super creamy, you can skip baking it and just put it under the broiler to brown the top. (Keep a close eye on it.) Then serve.

> I would like to take a moment to remember
> all of the delicious mac and cheese noodles
> I lost down the drain
> while I was trying to strain them.
> You deserved better.

Pasta Fruit Salad

8   oz. spiral pasta (or other pasta), cooked
¼   cup red onion, diced
1   cup strawberries, quartered
½   cup fresh blueberries
1   cup fresh or canned pineapple, cubed
1   cup poppy seed dressing
       spinach leaves
       pecans

Toss together first 6 ingredients. Serve on bed of spinach leaves and garnish with pecans.

Add some leftover ham or chicken to turn this dish into a full meal.

Bacon Jalapeno Poppers

½   cup cream cheese
½   cup sharp Cheddar cheese, shredded
6   slices bacon, cooked and crumbled
12   jalapeno peppers, halved lengthwise, seeds and membranes
         removed
6   slices uncooked bacon

Preheat oven to 400°. Line a baking sheet with aluminum foil.

Mix cream cheese, Cheddar cheese and bacon together in a bowl until evenly blended. Fill each jalapeno half with the cheese mixture. Wrap each with ½ piece of bacon. Place halves facing up on the prepared baking sheet.

Bake about 15 minutes.

Seasoned Noodle Mix

2 Tbsp. chicken bouillon granules
2 Tbsp. dried parsley
1 Tbsp. dried minced onion
¼ tsp. pepper

Mix and keep in air tight container.

This can be made with beef bouillon granules to use with beef dishes.

You can double, triple or quadruple this recipe to make it in bulk.

To Make Noodles

2 cups egg noodles, uncooked
1 tsp. butter or margarine
1¼ cup boiling water
5 tsp. seasoned noodle mix

Preheat oven to 350°. Place noodles in a greased 1 quart baking dish. Dot with butter. Add water and 5 teaspoons seasoned noodle mix. Cover and bake 15 minutes. Stir. Cover and bake 5 minutes longer or until noodles are tender. Let stand 5 minutes before serving.

- **Use plastic containers for your leftovers. Mark them with a dry erase pen so you will know when you put them in the fridge. It washes right off when you wash the container.**

Notes

Notes

Salads

Salad Tips

- **For quick and easy summer meals on hot days,** keep these things on hand. They're perfect for quick no-cook lunches and dinners:

  - A dozen or so boiled eggs

  - Cleaned lettuce, celery, broccoli and carrot sticks

  - Grated cheese

  - Lunch meat or sliced leftover meat

- **Make chef salads at least twice a week in the summer.** Chop up some of your cleaned carrot and celery sticks, slice hard boiled eggs, sliver some lunch meat and you have a chef salad. You can add any other vegetables you want, too.

- **Hard boiled eggs** make a great addition to tuna salad sandwiches. Serve on lettuce if you want a salad instead of a sandwich.

- **To make egg salad,** use a potato masher to chop the eggs.

- **Slice tomatoes vertically instead of horizontally** for a salad so the salad will stay firmer. This helps the dressing not get as watery.

- **Cooking in a hot kitchen is so much easier and faster** if everything is cleaned in advance.

- **If you use mayonnaise or dressings in a squeeze bottle** and want to get every last bit out of the jar, add a little milk to the bottle and shake it. Then pour it on something like potato salad. Do the same thing with ketchup, except add water, shake and pour into your spaghetti sauce.

- **When making gelatin salads with canned fruit,** don't throw the reserved juice away. Use part of it in place of the water you are supposed to use.

Mozzarella Dip

2   cups mayonnaise
1   cup (8 oz. container) sour cream
1   cup mozzarella cheese, grated
2   Tbsp. grated Parmesan cheese
1   tsp. onion powder
1   tsp. sugar
      dash garlic powder (to taste)
      seasoned salt (to taste)

Combine ingredients. Cover and chill for at least 1 hour. Serve with vegetables or tortilla chips.

Herb Dip

This dip tastes like some very expensive dips that you can buy pre-made. Be sure to use dried herbs and not powdered (except if using garlic powder). Dried herbs are the bigger flakes that haven't been ground fine.

1   clove crushed garlic or ½ tsp. garlic powder
2   (8 oz.) pkgs. cream cheese, softened
1   cup butter or margarine
1   tsp. dried oregano
1   tsp. Italian seasoning
¼   tsp. dill
¼   tsp. pepper

Blend all of the ingredients together. This herb dip will keep in the refrigerator for 1 week or in the freezer for 3 months.

Bacon Ranch Dip
The Best Dip You'll Ever Eat!

¾ cup ranch dressing
1   (8 oz.) pkg. cream cheese, softened
⅓ cup sour cream
1   cup Cheddar cheese, shredded
⅓ cup bacon bits, cooked
⅓ cup green onions, chopped
⅛ tsp. cayenne pepper (to taste, optional)

Preheat oven to 350°. Mix ranch dressing, cream cheese and sour cream until smooth. Stir in remaining ingredients.

Transfer into a ½ quart glass or stoneware baking dish.

Bake for about 15 minutes, until hot and bubbly at the edges underneath. Serve hot or warm, with veggies or crackers.

Cottage Cheese Dip

1½ cups (12 oz. package) cottage cheese
⅓ cup milk
1½ tsp. dried minced onion or ½ tsp. onion powder
½ tsp. seasoned salt
1   Tbsp. pimento, finely chopped
1   Tbsp. parsley, minced

Mix all of the ingredients together. Chill. This dip is especially good on a baked potato.

Guacamole

3   med. avocados, ripened
1   Tbsp. lime or lemon juice (or the juice of 1 lime)
1   tsp. garlic powder
1   tsp. onion powder (or ¼ cup onions, diced)
1   tsp. salt
¼-½ cup salsa (to taste) or ½ cup diced Roma tomatoes (optional)
      cilantro (optional, to taste)
      jalapeños (optional, to taste)

Slice avocados and scoop with a spoon into a medium bowl. Add lime or lemon juice. Add garlic, onion and salt. Mash avocados with a fork and stir until they are mixed together to the desired consistency. I usually make them fairly smooth, but you can leave bigger chunks if you like them that way. Stir in tomatoes, cilantro or jalapeños, if desired.

Easy Guacamole Tips

If you find avocados on sale, you can make a lot of homemade guacamole all at once, put the guacamole in smaller portions in ziplock bags and freeze. (I occasionally find fresh avocados on sale for 3 for $1.00.) When you're ready to use, simply defrost and serve.

If you slice the avocado in half and then make crosswise cuts in the avocado while it is still in the skin, it is easier to scoop. (It comes out in little cubes.)

To save time, use seasoned salt in place of garlic, onion and salt.

When you cut avocados, if there is a brown spot, cut it out and discard.

The lime juice is primarily to keep the guacamole from browning, but as long as it is being refrigerated, if it turns brown in the first day or two, it is usually still good, even though it is no longer pretty.

If you pour a layer of water over the top of fresh guacamole when you store it in the refrigerator, it will prevent browning. Drain off water and stir before serving.

Fresh Corn Salsa

4   tomatoes, chopped
1   cup (2 ears) fresh corn kernels, cooked
¼   cup onions, chopped
¼   cup fresh cilantro or parsley, chopped
1   jalapeno pepper, chopped
¼   cup Italian dressing

Mix everything well and serve.

Hummus

1   (15 oz.) can chickpeas or 1½ cups chickpeas, cooked
¼   cup fresh lemon juice (1 large lemon)
¼   cup tahini, well stirred (optional)
1   small clove garlic, minced (or more, to taste)
2   Tbsp. olive oil, plus more for serving
½   tsp. cumin
      salt (to taste)
2-3 Tbsp. water
      dash paprika (for serving)

Mix everything except paprika together in a blender, food processor or with a hand blender. Let sit at least 1 hour before serving. Just before serving, sprinkle olive oil and paprika on top.

I am really bad at measuring pasta, so if you and 79 of your friends would like to come to dinner tonight, that would be great.

Spicy Fruit Dip

1   (8 oz.) jar strawberry or raspberry preserves
2   cups (16 oz. jar) picante sauce
1   (8 oz.) pkg. cream cheese, softened

Mix preserves and picante sauce. Pour over the softened brick of cream cheese. Serve with tortilla chips or crackers.

Easy Fruit Dip

1   (8 oz.) pkg. cream cheese, softened
1   (14 oz.) can sweetened condensed milk
1   tsp. lemon juice

Take the cream cheese out of the refrigerator the night before so it is very soft. Whip with a mixer. Add condensed milk and lemon juice. Whip together.

Chef Salad

lettuce and/or spinach
cucumbers
carrots
tomatoes
ham, turkey or chicken
hard boiled eggs
diced shredded cheese
olives
croutons

Place shredded lettuce in a bowl. Top with desired vegetables, meat and toppings. You can add other veggies you would like to this salad too.

Confetti Salad

6   cups salad greens, cut into bite-size pieces
½   cup yellow pepper, chopped
½   cup red cabbage, shredded
1   cup mozzarella cheese, grated
      Italian dressing or dressing of your choice

Toss everything in a bowl and serve with dressing. Makes 8-10 servings.

• **If you have trouble chopping veggies like celery with a knife, try using scissors or a pizza cutter.**

Greek Salad

Dressing

¼   cup olive oil
2   Tbsp. plus 2 tsp. red wine vinegar
1   Tbsp. fresh dill
1   clove garlic, crushed
½   tsp. fresh oregano
⅛   tsp. salt
    dash of pepper

Salad

3   medium tomatoes, cut into wedges
3   medium green or yellow peppers, cut into strips
2   medium cucumbers, peeled and sliced
2   medium onions, chopped
1   cup (4 oz.) feta cheese
12   black olives
    anchovies (optional)

Whisk dressing in a large bowl. Add all of the veggies and coat well with dressing. Cover and chill 2 hours. Just before serving, add cheese, olives and anchovies, if desired.

Italian Garden Salad

2   medium cucumbers, peeled and sliced
1   cup cherry tomatoes, halved
1   cup red onion, sliced
½   cup green pepper, chopped
½   cup Italian salad dressing

Combine everything. Cover and chill until serving.

Garden Vegetable Salad

This salad is nice because you can prep the vegetables the night before or in the morning. Then you can toss it all together and let it set all day. By dinner time, it will be ready to set on the table -- one less thing to think about!

2	cups celery, sliced
2	cups cauliflower, sliced
2	cups cherry tomatoes, thinly sliced
2	cups carrots, halved
2	cups cucumbers, thinly sliced
1	medium onion, thinly sliced with the rings separated

Place vegetables in a large bowl.

Dressing

¾	cup olive or vegetable oil
½	cup fresh parsley, minced
3	Tbsp. white wine vinegar or cider vinegar
1	tsp. salt
1	tsp. ground mustard
⅛	tsp. pepper
1	clove garlic, minced

Place in jar with lid and shake to mix. Pour over vegetables and toss. Cover and refrigerate for at least 2 hours or overnight. Serve with a slotted spoon.

Bacon Pea Salad

1   (10 oz.) pkg. frozen peas, thawed
2   celery ribs, sliced
1   cup cauliflower, cut into small pieces
3   green onions, sliced
½   cup ranch dressing
¼   cup sour cream
4   bacon strips, cooked and crumbled
¼   cup sunflower seeds

Combine first four ingredients. Combine dressing and sour cream. Pour over salad and mix well. Cover and chill for 1 hour. Before serving, garnish with bacon and sunflower seeds.

- **Finely shred lettuce. People enjoy eating it more because they don't have to cut it or try stuffing huge pieces into their mouths.**

- **Keep it simple. Some of the best summer meals I ate were when I went to my grandma's house in Iowa. She would slice up some tomatoes, put sliced cucumbers in salt and vinegar water and set out some cottage cheese. For an extra hearty meal, she would add some soft bread with butter and apple butter. It was delicious.**

Cottage Cheese Spinach Salad

1   (10 oz.) bag fresh spinach
1   (12 oz.) container cottage cheese
½   cup pecans, chopped and roasted

Place all in a bowl and mix.

Dressing

½   cup sugar, to taste
3   Tbsp. vinegar
2   tsp. prepared horseradish
½   tsp. salt
½   tsp. ground mustard

Mix and drizzle on salad, tossing until well coated. Serve immediately.

Pimento Cottage Cheese

1   (16 oz.) container cottage cheese
1   small jar pimentos
1   cup Cheddar cheese, shredded
2-3 green onions, chopped

Mix everything and serve.

• **When you have a salad recipe that includes a special dressing, mix the dressing in the bottom of the bowl you will use to serve the salad. When it comes time to make the salad, just place the salad ingredients on top of the dressing and toss. This prevents you from dirtying an extra bowl.**

Mushroom Spinach Salad

8   cups fresh spinach
½   lb. fresh mushrooms, sliced
4   green onions, chopped
6   bacon strips
2   Tbsp. lemon juice
2   Tbsp. water
½   tsp. ground mustard
¼   tsp. pepper
3   hard boiled eggs, cut into large chunks

Combine spinach, mushrooms and onions. Fry bacon and remove from pan.

Add everything else but the eggs to the bacon drippings in the pan and heat through. Drizzle over salad. Sprinkle with eggs and crumble bacon on top.

BLT Pasta Salad

This recipe has no real measurements. You can add as little or much of each ingredient as you like.

spiral pasta (or your favorite pasta)
cooked bacon, cooked and crumbled
tomatoes, chopped
mayonnaise or Miracle Whip dressing
lettuce

Mix pasta, bacon and tomatoes together and toss with dressing. Serve on a bed of lettuce.

Cucumber Salad

3   medium cucumbers, peeled, diced or sliced
½   medium onion, diced or sliced
1   Tbsp. white vinegar
⅓   cup sugar
¼   cup water

Mix everything. Cover and refrigerate several hours or overnight. Serves 4.

Crispy Cucumber Salad

4   large cucumbers, peeled and cut into 1 inch cubes
6   radishes, thinly sliced
1   large tomato, cut into bite-size chunks
¼   cup red onion, chopped
⅓   cup pitted ripe olives
1-2 Tbsp. fresh basil
½   cup feta cheese, crumbled
⅓   cup Italian dressing

Toss everything together and serve.

- **Cutting your salads or veggies into different shapes can quickly turn a "Ho hum" salad into an "Oh yum" salad. Slice your carrots into coins or grate them. Cut your peppers into strips instead of dicing them. Slice cucumbers into circles or if that's what you usually do, try dicing them.**

Tomato Cucumber Salad

2-3   tomatoes, cubed
2-3   cucumbers, cubed
         fresh dill (to taste)
         salt and pepper (to taste)
2   Tbsp. sour cream

Mix ingredients and serve.

Chow Mein Noodle Salad

4   cups lettuce, shredded
1   cup chow mein noodles
⅔   cup chicken breast, cooked and cubed
2   green onions, chopped
4   tsp. sliced almonds, toasted
4   tsp. sesame seeds, toasted

Vinaigrette

¼   cup olive oil or canola oil
4½   tsp. white wine vinegar
1   Tbsp. sugar
¼   tsp. pepper
⅛   tsp. salt

In a large salad bowl, combine the lettuce, chow mein noodles, chicken, onions, almonds and sesame seeds.

In a jar with a tight fitting lid, combine the vinaigrette ingredients and shake well. Drizzle over salad and toss to coat.

Broccoli Salad

This dressing is also great for a coleslaw dressing.

2   bunches fresh broccoli florets
1   bunch green onions, chopped
1   cup raisins (white or regular)
1   cup sunflower seeds
     bacon bits

Dressing

1   cup mayonnaise
½   cup sugar

Mix broccoli, onions, and raisins. Mix dressing. Pour over broccoli mix and chill. Just before serving, sprinkle with sunflower seeds and bacon bits.

Feel free to adjust this salad. Use less or no dressing for fewer calories.

Broccoli Avocado Salad

4   cups broccoli, cut into pieces
4   cups cauliflower, cut into pieces
2   cups celery, sliced
½   cup green olives, sliced
1   avocado, cut into small cubes
¼-½ cup sunflower seeds
     Italian dressing

Put all ingredients into a bowl and sprinkle with Italian dressing, to taste. You can prepare everything the previous day except the avocado and dressing.

Marinated Tomato Salad

Marinade

¼   cup oil
1   Tbsp. sugar
3   Tbsp. vinegar
2   tsp. parsley, finely chopped
1   tsp. green onion, finely chopped
⅛   tsp. garlic salt
⅛   tsp. basil
1   dash dried oregano
1   dash pepper

Salad

12   cherry tomatoes
4   cups lettuce, torn
2   oz. Swiss cheese slices, cut into strips
½   cup croutons

In a large bowl, mix the marinade ingredients. Add the tomatoes and toss to coat. Cover and chill 8 hours or overnight.

Just before serving, drain the tomatoes, reserving the marinade.

To serve, add lettuce and cheese to the tomatoes. Add enough marinade to moisten. Add croutons just before serving.

• **When you have leftover tomatoes or other veggies, make a puree of them and freeze in ice cube trays. After they are frozen, put them in a plastic bag. The next time you make soup or stew or need them for seasoning something, use only as many cubes as you need.**

Grandma's Fruit Salad

1   cup grapes, halved
1   (11 oz.) can mandarin oranges
1   apple, cored and cut into cubes
1   banana, sliced
¼   cup sugar
½   cup walnuts, chopped
1   (8 oz.) container whipped topping

Place all of the fruit in a bowl. Sprinkle with sugar and walnuts. Add whipped cream. Gently stir until mixed and serve.

Pear Fruit Compote

¼   cup brown sugar, packed
1   tsp. cornstarch
¼   cup water
¼   cup concentrated orange juice
2   Tbsp. butter or margarine
1   (20 oz.) can pineapple chunks, drained
1   (15¼ oz.) can pear halves, drained
1   (15 oz.) can mandarin oranges, drained

Topping

1   (3 oz.) pkg. cream cheese, softened
1   Tbsp. sugar
1   Tbsp. concentrated orange juice

In a large saucepan, combine the first 5 ingredients in order. Bring to a boil and cook for 2 minutes, until thickened. Add fruit, turn down heat and just heat through. In a small bowl, beat topping ingredients until smooth. Serve fruit with a dollop of topping.

Orange Ambrosia

⅓   cup granola cereal (without raisins)
⅓   cup walnuts, chopped
⅓   cup coconut
4   (6 oz.) cartons orange yogurt
1   banana, sliced
1   (11 oz.) can mandarin oranges, drained.

Mix cereal, nuts, and coconut. In 4 bowls or parfait glasses, layer
½ container yogurt, fruit and 2 Tbsp. of cereal mix for each bowl. Layer
again and garnish with oranges. Serve immediately. Serves 4.

Double Crunch
Apple Salad

1   large golden or green apple, cut in bite-size pieces
1   large red apple, cut in bite-size pieces
1   tsp. lemon juice
1   (20 oz.) can pineapple chunks, drained
1   cup miniature marshmallows
⅔   cup flaked coconut
½   cup nuts
1   small container whipped topping

Toss apples with lemon juice. Add the rest of the ingredients. If you don't
have any whipped topping or want a more savory salad, replace the
whipped topping with ¼ cup mayo and 2 tablespoons each of celery and
raisins.

• **When you can, eat the peel on your apple. That is where ⅔ of the
  fiber is found.**

Strawberry Salad With Poppy Seed Dressing

¼ cup sugar
⅓ cup slivered almonds
1 bunch romaine lettuce, torn (about 8 cups) or spinach
1 small onion, halved and thinly sliced
2 cups fresh strawberries, halved

Dressing

¼ cup mayonnaise
2 Tbsp. sugar
1 Tbsp. sour cream
1 Tbsp. milk
2¼ tsp. cider vinegar
1½ tsp. poppy seeds
½ tsp. garlic powder

Pour sugar into a small heavy skillet. Cook and stir over medium-low heat until melted and caramel colored, about 10 minutes. Stir in almonds until coated. Spread on foil to cool.

Place romaine, onion and strawberries in a large bowl. Whisk together dressing ingredients. Toss with salad. Break candied almonds into pieces. Sprinkle over salad. Serve immediately.

For A Main Dish: Grill 2 pounds boneless skinless chicken breasts, slice and add to the salad for 10 main dish servings.

Didn't severely cut myself or burn myself.
It was a good day.

Vinegar Coleslaw

1   head green cabbage, finely shredded
1   large carrot, grated
½   yellow or red onion, finely sliced (optional)

Dressing

⅓   cup white or apple cider vinegar
3   Tbsp. olive oil
1   Tbsp. sugar or honey, (or more, depending on sweetness)
½   Tbsp. Dijon mustard (optional)
      salt and pepper (to taste)

Mix cabbage, carrot and onion in a large bowl.

Whisk dressing ingredients together in a small bowl. Taste the dressing and decide if you'd like to add more sweetener.

Add about half of the dressing to the cabbage, carrots and onions and gently toss. Slowly add more dressing, to taste.

- **Use leftover dill pickle juice in potato salad, coleslaw, salad dressings or any recipes that call for vinegar.**

- **Dill pickle is especially good in potato salad.**

- **To keep salad crisp, place a saucer upside down in the bowl before adding salad. The water will drain and stay under the saucer.**

Dorothy Lynch® Dressing Copycat

1	cup olive, canola or vegetable oil
¾	cup sugar
1	(10¾ oz.) can Campbell's tomato soup*
½	cup vinegar
⅛	tsp. garlic powder
1	tsp. dry mustard
1	tsp. salt
1	tsp. celery seed
⅛	tsp. pepper
1	Tbsp. cornstarch

Mix all ingredients in a blender until creamy. Pour into a canning jar or container and refrigerate overnight.

*In this case, Campbell's soup does taste better.

Honey Mustard Dressing

1	cup mayonnaise
¼	cup prepared mustard
¼	cup honey
1	Tbsp. apple cider vinegar

In a small bowl, whisk together all ingredients. Store, covered, in the refrigerator.

Chunky Blue Cheese Dressing

⅓   cup buttermilk or milk
1   tsp. white vinegar
5   oz. blue cheese, crumbled
⅓   cup + 1 Tbsp. sour cream
¼   cup mayonnaise
4   tsp. white wine vinegar
½   tsp. sugar
¼   tsp. garlic powder
⅛   tsp. pepper
     dash salt

In a medium bowl, mix buttermilk and white vinegar. Let sit for 5 minutes.

Stir. Add remaining ingredients and mash with a fork until well combined. Pour into a mason jar or other container and seal tightly. Let set in fridge for at least 4 hours. Will last 4 weeks.

Balsamic Dijon Dressing

3   Tbsp. Dijon mustard
3   Tbsp. honey
     salt (to taste)
     pepper (to taste)
1   cup olive oil
1   cup balsamic vinegar

Place the ingredients in a mason jar. Screw the lid on tightly and shake vigorously. The dressing can remain in the fridge for 1-2 weeks.

Greek Salad Dressing

4	cloves garlic (minced)
2	tsp. Dijon mustard
2	Tbsp. lemon juice
1	tsp. lemon zest
1	tsp. sugar or honey (optional)
¼	cup red wine vinegar
¼	tsp. dried basil
½	tsp. dried oregano
⅛	tsp. salt (to taste)
¼	tsp. pepper
1	cup olive oil

Add all ingredients except oil to a blender. Pulse several times to mix ingredients. With blender running on high, slowly pour oil into blender until mixture is creamy. Transfer to a jar with a lid. Cover with the lid and refrigerate up to 2 weeks.

Chili-Lime Dressing

	zest and juice of 2 limes (4 Tbsp. juice and 1 Tbsp. zest)
¼	cup red wine vinegar
1	Tbsp. soy sauce
1	Tbsp. honey
⅓	cup olive oil
1	clove garlic, finely minced or 1 tsp. garlic powder
½	tsp. red pepper flakes
1	tsp. ground cumin
½	tsp. salt

Place ingredients in a mason jar. Screw the lid on tightly and shake vigorously. The dressing can be refrigerated for 1-2 weeks.

Notes

Notes

Main Dishes

Meat Tips

- **It is great to have extra meatballs already made and in the freezer** so you can use your crockpot on hot days.

- **Keep packages of French onion dip in your pantry.** For a great flavor enhancement, add a tablespoon of the dip mix to homemade macaroni and cheese, sprinkle on cooked veggies, mix into meatloaf or hamburger patties or just sprinkle on different meats. Try some sprinkled on homemade (or canned) dinner rolls or mixed in to your favorite potato recipe.

- **Save dry, stale bread to soak up grease from fried meat.** Let it dry out after you soak up the grease. Crumble and feed to the birds.

- **Cut meat with kitchen shears.** It takes half as long as cutting with a knife and you don't have to clean a cutting board afterward.

- **If you are cutting something like steak into cubes with a knife,** cut it when it's slightly frozen, because it is easier to cut.

- **Add salt to flour before using it to make gravy.** The salt will help prevent gravy from lumping as much.

- **If you use a lot of caramelized onions,** make some extra and freeze for the next time you need them. They last 3 months in the freezer.

Just salad for me for dinner please. A vanilla ice cream salad with hot fudge dressing and crouton marshmallows.

One Pan Homemade Hamburger Helper

½   lb. ground beef
4   cups water
1   cup regular elbow macaroni, uncooked
1   tsp. onion powder
½   tsp. garlic powder
1   tsp. chili powder
½   cup tomato paste
2   beef bouillon cubes
    salt and pepper (to taste)
    cheese, grated (optional)
    parsley (optional)

Brown ground beef in a skillet. Drain off the fat, and add remaining ingredients to the skillet.

Stir to combine. Bring to a boil and simmer, uncovered, for about 15 minutes or until it reaches desired thickness. Season with salt and pepper. Garnish with cheese and parsley, if desired.

"Honey, can you pick up pizza? I have been busy Pinning nutritious recipes for our family all day."

Beef Brisket

3-4   lb. beef brisket
1   Tbsp. vegetable oil

Rub

1   Tbsp. brown sugar
2   tsp. paprika
1   tsp. onion powder
1   tsp. garlic powder
½   tsp. cumin
¾   tsp. mustard powder
1   tsp. salt
½   tsp. pepper

Mix rub ingredients. Rub all over brisket. If time permits, leave for 30 minutes to 24 hours in the fridge.

Barbecue Sauce

2   cloves garlic, minced or 2 tsp. minced garlic
½   cup apple cider vinegar
1½   cups ketchup
½   cup brown sugar, packed
2   tsp. pepper
2   tsp. onion powder
2   tsp. mustard powder
1   tsp. cayenne pepper (to taste)
1   Tbsp. Worcestershire sauce
1   tsp. Liquid Smoke seasoning

Combine all ingredients and serve.

Beef Brisket (continued)

For Crockpot

Combine barbecue sauce ingredients in a crockpot. Mix.

Add brisket. You may need to stuff it in. It will shrink as it cooks. Slow cook on low in crockpot for 8-10 hours. Remove brisket onto a tray.

For Oven

Mix barbecue sauce ingredients in a large baking pan that fits your brisket. Add brisket.

Bake, covered with foil, 8-10 hours at 275°. Remove brisket onto a tray.

To serve: Slice brisket thinly across the grain and serve with barbecue sauce.

Slow Cooked Cranberry Roast

1	(3 lb.) chuck roast
1	(1 oz.) pkg. dry onion soup mix
1	(16 oz.) can jellied cranberry sauce
½	cup water
1	Tbsp. cornstarch (to thicken gravy)

Place roast in crockpot. Sprinkle with onion soup mix and place cranberry sauce on top. Add water. Cover and cook 8 hours on low.

Remove meat from the crockpot. To thicken the gravy, make a thin paste of 1 tablespoon of cornstarch and water. Whisk into the juices, turn on high and bring to a boil.

If you want, you can add some baby carrots and quartered potatoes during the last 4 hours of cooking.

Beef And Broccoli

3   Tbsp. cornstarch, divided
3   Tbsp. water
1   lb. flank steak, round steak, leftover roast beef or chicken,
        cut into 1 inch pieces
½   cup soy sauce
3   Tbsp. brown sugar, packed
3   cloves garlic, minced or 1 Tbsp. minced garlic
2   tsp. fresh ginger, grated
2   Tbsp. vegetable oil, divided
4   cups small broccoli florets
½   cup white onions, sliced

In a large bowl, whisk together 2 tablespoons cornstarch with
3 tablespoons water. Add the beef to the bowl and toss to combine. In a
separate small bowl, whisk together the remaining 1 tablespoon
cornstarch with the soy sauce, brown sugar, garlic and ginger. Set the
sauce aside.

Heat 1 tablespoon of the vegetable oil in a large nonstick sauté pan over
medium heat. Once it is hot, add the beef and cook, stirring constantly
until the beef is half cooked through.

Add the remaining 1 tablespoon of vegetable oil to the pan. Once it is hot,
add the broccoli florets and sliced onions and cook, stirring occasionally,
until the broccoli is tender, about 4 minutes. Add the prepared sauce.
Bring the mixture to a boil and cook, stirring, for 1 minute or until the
sauce thickens slightly. Serve with rice or noodles.

Advice is like cooking. You should try it
first before you feed it to others.

Bacon Cheese Meatloaf

1	egg
¼	cup evaporated milk
1½	cups Swiss cheese, grated
1	cup bacon, cooked and crumbled (about 10 slices)
½	cup soft bread crumbs (leftover dinner rolls are especially good for bread crumbs)
½	tsp. garlic powder
½	tsp. onion powder
1½	lbs. ground beef

Preheat oven to 350°. Combine everything except ½ cup of the Swiss cheese and ¼ cup of the bacon. Mix well and shape into a loaf. Place the loaf into a greased loaf pan or baking dish. Bake, uncovered, for 1 hour.

Drain. Sprinkle with the remaining cheese and bacon and bake 5 minutes longer or until the cheese is melted. Let stand for 10 minutes before slicing.

• Shake the crumbs out of your bread bag next time you finish a loaf and place it in a container. Then, when you make something messy like meatloaf, mix it in the bread bag and just toss it away. No clean up needed. You can also use bread bags to roll out graham cracker crumbs or soda cracker crumbs.

• Leftover Meatloaf? Grind or chop leftover roast or meatloaf. Add a little onion, ketchup or tomato paste and use it as a filling for stuffed, baked green peppers.

Extraordinary Meatloaf

1   lb. ground beef
1   lb. sausage (spicy if you like it)
1   cup bread crumbs
2   Tbsp. Worcestershire sauce
2   eggs
1   tsp. salt
¼   tsp. pepper
3   cups Colby cheese, grated

Preheat oven to 400°. Mix all of the ingredients and place in a loaf pan.
Bake 45 minutes.

Instead of pouring ketchup on top of your meatloaf, try this glaze:

Meatloaf Glaze

¼   cup brown sugar
1   Tbsp. Dijon mustard
1   tsp. apple cider vinegar

Mix the ingredients and pour on the meatloaf about 15 minutes before it is
done.

Using this meatloaf recipe, make meatballs to serve at a Super Bowl
party. This is a delicious alternative to the regular barbecue meatballs. If
you use the recipe to make meatballs, turn the oven temperature down to
375°.

Christmas Meatballs

2   lbs. ground beef
1   pkg. Stove Top stuffing for chicken
1   cup water
2   eggs
1   (18 oz.) bottle barbecue sauce
1   (16 oz.) can cranberry sauce

Preheat oven to 400°. Line two 15x10x1 inch jelly roll pans with foil and spray with cooking spray. Mix the first 4 ingredients. Shape into balls the size of walnuts and place on pans. Bake 15-20 minutes, until done.

While the meatballs are baking, mix the barbecue sauce and the cranberry sauce in a large saucepan and bring to a boil, stirring occasionally. Add the meatballs to sauce and coat evenly.

The meatballs from this recipe can be frozen in a plastic bag. Lay the bag flat in the freezer to make the meatballs freeze individually. They will keep for up to 3 months.

These meatballs are handy to keep on hand to take to a last minute activity, whether it is tailgating, a Christmas or New Year's get together or as an appetizer for unexpected company.

- **When you make a meatloaf or meatballs, make extra and keep them in the freezer for another quick meal.**

- **There are many different meals you can make with frozen meatballs:**
  - **Spaghetti**
  - **Meatball sandwiches**
  - **Barbecued meatballs**
  - **Meatballs served by themselves as the main meat**
  - **Add cream sauce for Swedish meatballs.**
  - **Sweet and sour sauce meatballs**

Meatball Stew

You can adjust the vegetables to use whatever you have on hand.

3   potatoes, peeled and cubed
1   (16 oz.) pkg. fresh baby carrots, quartered
1   large onion, chopped
3   celery ribs, sliced
1   (12 oz.) pkg. frozen cooked meatballs
1   (10½ oz.) can tomato soup, undiluted
1   cup water
1   (10½ oz.) can beef gravy*
1   envelope onion soup mix
2   tsp. beef bouillon granules

Layer the first 5 ingredients in a 5 quart crockpot. Mix the remaining ingredients together and pour over the meatballs and vegetables. Cover and cook on low for 9-10 hours or until vegetables are tender. Makes 6 servings.

*You can freeze gravy, so the next time you have one or two lone cups of leftover gravy, freeze it and save it to use for this recipe.

Mini Burgers

1   lb. ground beef
1   (8 oz.) pkg. Cheddar cheese, shredded
1   Tbsp. mayonnaise
1   (1 oz.) pkg. dry onion soup mix
24   (2 inch square) dinner rolls, split

Preheat oven to 350°. Mix everything but the dinner rolls. Spread even amounts of ground beef mix on the bottom half of rolls. Place the top halves on top of the meat mix, making sandwiches. If your rolls came in a foil pan, then put them back on the pan. If not, then place on a baking sheet and cover tightly with foil. Bake for 30-35 minutes, until the meat is cooked through.

13 Easy Roll Ups

1   uncooked pizza crust* or
      ½ batch 90 Minute Amish Bread dough (p. 88)
      filling ingredients of your choice (see below)

Preheat oven to 400°. Pre-cook meat and vegetable ingredients. Roll pizza crust into an 8x15 inch rectangle and spread with desired fillings. Roll like you would cinnamon rolls and crimp edges. Lay, seam side down, on a greased baking sheet. Bake 20-25 minutes.

*You can buy already made pizza crust or make your own pizza crust.

Variations

- **Burger:** Hamburger and onions. Serve with pickles, mustard, ketchup and mayonnaise.

- **Cheeseburger:** Burger above plus American cheese.

- **Bacon Cheeseburger:** Bacon, hamburger, onions, Velveeta cheese.

- **Pizza:** Add pizza sauce, mozzarella cheese, favorite pizza toppings

- **Barbecue Chicken:** Barbecue sauce and chicken

- **Artichoke Chicken:** pesto sauce, artichokes, chicken and Parmesan cheese

- **Ham and cheese:** diced ham and Swiss cheese

- **Veggie:** garlic sauce with sauteed vegetables

- **Philly Cheesesteak:** steak strips, sliced peppers, white Cheddar or provolone cheese

- **Hawaiian:** Canadian bacon, pineapple, mozzarella cheese

- **Greek:** Black olives, artichoke hearts, red onion, feta

- **Meat:** Sausage, salami, Italian sausage, Canadian bacon and/or any meat you like

- **Breakfast:** American cheese, eggs, bacon or sausage

Taco Meat Filling

1   lb. ground beef*
½   cup tomato sauce
1   pkg. taco seasoning or 5 tsp. homemade taco seasoning**

Cook the ground beef fully. Drain grease. Then add tomato sauce and taco seasoning. Simmer 5 minutes.

* Shredded chicken may be used instead.

** **Homemade taco seasoning:** 1 Tbsp. chili powder, ¾ tsp. cumin, ½ tsp. dried oregano, ¼ tsp. garlic powder, ¼ tsp. onion powder, ½ tsp. salt

Tacos

12   taco shells
½   lb. taco meat filling
2   (15 oz.) cans refried beans or 3½ cups refried beans, homemade
½   head iceberg lettuce, thinly sliced
2   medium tomatoes, chopped
1-2   avocados, chopped peeled and pitted, or guacamole
3   oz. cheese, grated
1   cup salsa, or ½ cup sliced pickled jalapeños
     handful fresh cilantro, chopped

Warm taco shells in the oven or microwave.

Oven: Warm taco shells at 350° for 5 minutes.

Microwave: Warm taco shells 10-15 seconds for 3 shells. Layer ingredients in shells and enjoy.

Taco Salad

1   bag tortilla chips
½   head iceberg lettuce, thinly sliced
½   lb. taco meat filling (p. 226)
2   (15 oz.) cans refried beans or 3½ cups refried beans, homemade
2   medium tomatoes, chopped
1-2 avocados, chopped peeled and pitted, or guacamole
3   oz. cheese, grated
1   cup salsa, or ½ cup sliced pickled jalapeños
      handful fresh cilantro, chopped

Lay a single layer of chips on plate. Layer ingredients in order given dividing between plates. Serve and enjoy. Serves 6-8.

Taco Pasta Bake

4-6 cups pasta, cooked (can use macaroni, spiral or any kind)
1   cup taco meat filling* (p. 226)
4   oz. cream cheese, softened
1½   cup Cheddar cheese, grated (or Mexican mix)

Preheat oven to 350°. Stir taco meat filling and cream cheese together. In a casserole dish mix pasta, taco filling mixture and cheese (reserving ½ cup to sprinkle on top). Bake, uncovered, for 30 minutes.

Sprinkle remaining cheese on top.

*1 lb. ground beef and 1 pkg. taco seasoning may be used instead.

Tostadas

12   tostada shells
½   lb. taco meat filling (p. 226)
2   (15 oz.) cans refried beans or 3½ cups refried beans, homemade
½   head iceberg lettuce, thinly sliced
2   medium tomatoes, chopped
1-2   avocados, chopped peeled and pitted, or guacamole
3   oz. cheese, grated
1   cup salsa, or ½ cup sliced pickled jalapeños
      fresh cilantro, chopped (optional)

Warm tostada shells in the oven or microwave.

Oven: 350° for 5 minutes.

Microwave: 10-15 seconds for 3 shells. Layer ingredients on shells and enjoy.

Burritos

6-8   large soft flour tortillas or round wraps
½   lb. taco meat filling (p. 226)
3   cups cooked rice, warm
3   cups iceberg lettuce, thinly sliced
1   cup black beans
3   tomatoes, diced
½   red onion, finely chopped
      fresh cilantro, chopped (optional)
1½   cups cheese, shredded

Warm tortillas in microwave between two wet paper towels. Layer ingredients into each tortilla as desired. Fold bottom up to cover filling and tightly roll.

Easy Enchiladas

½   lb. ground beef, cooked* or taco meat filling (p. 226)
1   (15 oz.) can pinto beans, drained
1   (15 oz.) can enchilada sauce
2   cups Cheddar cheese, grated and divided
1   (4 oz.) can chopped green chilies
1½ cups corn chips, crushed
1   tsp. onion powder
1   cup sour cream
    additional corn chips (for dipping)

Mix everything but 1 cup of the cheese and the sour cream. Cover and microwave on high for 3 minutes, stirring once. Top with the rest of the cheese and the sour cream. Uncover and heat again until the cheese is melted, about 1-2 minutes. Serve with chips.

*If you don't have ground beef already cooked, you can cook it in a pan on the stovetop. Then drain the browned beef, add the rest of the ingredients and warm through so you only use one pan.

A recent study found that women
who carry a little extra weight
live longer than men who mention it.

Creamy Chicken Enchiladas

10   flour tortillas
2   cups chicken, cooked and shredded
2   cups Monterey Jack cheese, grated (Cheddar or mozzarella is OK)
     salt and pepper (to taste)
2   Tbsp. butter, melted
2   Tbsp. all purpose flour
2   cups chicken broth
1   cup sour cream
1   (4 oz.) can green chilies

Preheat oven to 350°. Mix chicken, 1 cup cheese, salt and pepper. Spread on tortillas. Roll tortillas and place, seam side down, in a 9x13 inch pan.

Melt butter in a saucepan. Stir in flour. Simmer 1 minute, stirring constantly, until thickened. Whisk in chicken broth, stirring until smooth. Add sour cream and green chilies. Warm through. Do not boil.

Pour sauce over tortillas and sprinkle with remaining cheese.
Bake 20-25 minutes.

- **Did your tortillas get dried out? Don't toss them. Crumble them into small pieces after they are dry and add to soups or salads in place of croutons.**

7 Layer Taco Dip

1	(16 oz.) can refried beans
2	Tbsp. milk
1	(8 oz.) pkg. cream cheese, softened
½	cup sour cream
2	Tbsp. taco seasoning
1	cup prepared guacamole
1¼	cups salsa, drained
1½	cups Cheddar cheese
½	cup black olives or tomatoes (You can use both.)
4	green onions, sliced

Combine refried beans and milk (or you can use the liquid from the salsa if you prefer) until smooth. Spread on the bottom of a tray.

Combine cream cheese, sour cream and taco seasoning with a mixer on medium. Spread over refried beans.

Spoon guacamole over cream cheese and gently spread. Repeat with drained salsa. Top with cheese, olives, tomatoes and green onions.

Chill 1 hour before serving. Serve with tortilla chips or crackers.

> You know your life has changed
> when going to the grocery store
> by yourself is a vacation.

Oven Fried Chicken With Biscuits

It's okay to lay the biscuits in the margarine in the bottom of the pan. That makes the biscuits crispy. Oh, yum!

4-5	Tbsp. margarine (not butter)
½	cup baking mix (Bisquick)
4-6	pieces of chicken
	salt and pepper (to taste)
1	can refrigerator biscuits

Preheat oven to 375°. Melt margarine in a 9x13 inch pan. Pour the baking mix on a plate or in a plastic bag. Roll the chicken in the margarine, then into the baking mix and place back into the pan. Salt and pepper, to taste. Bake 45 minutes, until the juices run clear.

About 5-10 minutes before the chicken is done, push the pieces of chicken tightly against one side of the pan and lay the biscuits into the pan on the opposite side. Finish baking until the biscuits are brown.

Parmesan Chicken Tenders

2-3	lbs. boneless, skinless chicken, cut into strips
1	egg, beaten
	grated Parmesan cheese
	frying oil

Roll strips of chicken in beaten egg; then roll in Parmesan cheese. Fry in your favorite oil.

Garlic Chicken

¼   cup olive oil
2   cloves garlic, minced or 2 tsp. minced garlic
¼   cup Italian seasoned bread crumbs
¼   cup grated Parmesan cheese
2   boneless, skinless chicken breasts, halved

Preheat oven to 425°. Heat olive oil and garlic in a small saucepan over low heat until warmed, 1 to 2 minutes. Transfer garlic and oil to a shallow bowl. Combine bread crumbs and Parmesan cheese in a separate shallow bowl.

Dip chicken breast halves in the olive oil and garlic mixture. Then dip into the bread crumb mixture and turn to evenly coat. Place into a shallow baking dish.

Bake 30 to 35 minutes, until chicken is no longer pink and juices run clear. A thermometer inserted into the center should read at least 165°.

40 Clove Garlic Chicken

4   chicken thighs or breasts, with skin
       salt and pepper (to taste)
½   cup plus 2 Tbsp. olive oil
1   tsp. thyme
40   peeled cloves garlic, about 2 bulbs

Preheat oven to 350°. Season chicken with salt and pepper. In an oven-proof skillet, add 2 tablespoons olive oil and brown chicken on both sides over high heat.

Remove from heat, Add ½ cup oil, thyme and garlic cloves. Cover and bake 1½ hours. Remove chicken from the oven. Let rest for 5 to 10 minutes.

Honey Garlic Chicken

2   tsp. vegetable oil
1½   lbs. boneless, skinless chicken breasts or thighs,
        cut into small pieces (about ½ inch)
     salt and pepper (to taste)
3   Tbsp. honey
3   Tbsp. soy sauce
3   cloves garlic, minced or 1 Tbsp. minced garlic
¼   tsp. red pepper flakes (optional, to taste)

For Serving (optional)

- brown rice
- green onions, sliced
- sesame seeds
- lime wedges to squeeze over chicken

Heat olive oil in a large skillet over medium-high heat. Lightly season the chicken with salt and pepper. Add the chicken to the skillet and brown on one side, about 3-4 minutes.

Meanwhile, make the sauce. Whisk the honey, soy sauce, garlic and red pepper flakes, if using, in a small bowl until well combined. Add the sauce to the pan and toss to coat the chicken pieces. Cook until chicken is cooked through, 4-5 more minutes.

Serve with steamed rice and top with green onions, sesame seeds and a squeeze of lime juice, if desired.

- **Don't wash chicken- it just splats germs all over your kitchen. No self respecting germ would live through a proper cooking of chicken, so don't make your family sick by spreading chicken juice all over. (The CDC agrees with us.)**

Chinese Chicken Base

(Thanks to my sister in law, Sheala, for this recipe.)

1½-2 lbs. boneless chicken breast, cut into ¾ inch cubes
1   cup flour
½   cup cornstarch
2   tsp. baking powder
1   tsp. baking soda
1¼   cups cold water

In a medium frying pan, heat oil on high (at least 1 inch deep in pan) until hot.

In a medium mixing bowl, combine flour, cornstarch, baking powder, baking soda and water until smooth in consistency. Add chicken to batter and stir until coated.

Drop coated pieces individually into hot oil, frying until cooked. (Otherwise, they will clump together.)

If you like, for a little extra flavor and color, you can also lightly sauté your choice of veggies like bell peppers, chunks of white onions and carrots and add them to your choice of sauce at the end, pouring a little extra sauce over the top when the veggies are added.

(Sauce options are in the next several recipes.)

- **When frying something that needs more oil, slowly add the oil at the edge of the pan. This will cause it to heat to the perfect temperature before it hits the food.**

- **To tell if your oil is hot enough when frying, stick a wooden skewer or wooden spoon handle in the oil. If bubbles form around it, then the oil is ready.**

- **Try using pancake mix in place of flour for a different flavor when coating and frying something.**

Sweet And Sour Chicken

¼ cup cornstarch
½ cup water
⅓ cup pineapple juice
½ cup brown sugar
½ cup sugar
½ cup apple cider vinegar
½ cup ketchup
1 Tbsp. soy sauce
2 lbs. Chinese chicken base (p. 239)

In a medium pot, add ingredients, except chicken base, and stir. Cook for 5 minutes, until the mixture begins to thicken. Pour over chicken.

Sesame Chicken

¼ cup soy sauce
2 Tbsp. water
1 Tbsp. oil, butter or margarine
3 Tbsp. brown sugar
1 Tbsp. rice vinegar
1 tsp. fresh ginger, grated
2 cloves garlic, minced or 2 tsp. minced garlic
1 Tbsp. sesame seeds
½ Tbsp. cornstarch
2 lbs. Chinese chicken base (p. 239)

In a medium pot, add ingredients, except chicken base, and stir. Cook for 5 minutes, until the mixture begins to thicken. Pour over chicken.

Chinese Garlic Chicken

2   Tbsp. brown sugar
¼   cup soy sauce
1   Tbsp. white vinegar or rice vinegar
1   cup vegetable broth or water
1½   Tbsp. cornstarch
2   Tbsp. canola oil
1   tsp. onion powder
3   Tbsp. garlic, chopped or 1 tsp. garlic powder
1   Tbsp. ginger, chopped or 1 tsp. ginger powder
2   lbs. Chinese chicken base (p. 239)

In a medium pot, add ingredients, except chicken base, and stir. Cook for 5 minutes, until the mixture begins to thicken. Pour over chicken.

Orange Chicken

1   cup orange juice
½   cup sugar
2   Tbsp. rice vinegar or white vinegar
2   Tbsp. soy sauce
¼   tsp. ginger powder or 1 tsp. ginger, chopped
¼   tsp. garlic powder or 2 cloves garlic, minced or 2 tsp. minced garlic
½   tsp. red chili flakes
1   Tbsp. cornstarch
     orange zest from 1 orange
2   lbs. Chinese chicken base (p. 239)

In a medium pot, add ingredients, except orange zest and chicken base, and stir. Cook for 5 minutes, until the mixture begins to thicken. Once the sauce is thickened, remove from heat and add orange zest. Pour over chicken.

Lemon Chicken

1   (3½ lb.) chicken
1½ tsp. lemon pepper seasoning (p. 340)
1½ tsp. seasoned salt
½   tsp. thyme
1   medium lemon, halved
2   fresh rosemary sprigs (You can also use dried.)

Loosen skin around the chicken breast, leg and thigh, being careful not to tear the skin. Combine the seasonings. Rub half under the skin. Cut half of the lemon into quarters and place in the cavity along with the rosemary sprigs.

Place chicken, breast down, in a roasting pan. Squeeze the remaining lemon over the chicken. Rub the chicken with the remaining spice mixture.

Bake, uncovered, at 375° for 1 to 1½ hours, until the chicken juices run clear or a meat thermometer inserted in the thigh reads 180°. (Cover loosely with foil if you notice it is browning too quickly.)
After baking, cover and let stand 15 minutes.

Apricot Chicken

1   lb. boneless, skinless chicken breast or thighs, cut into chunks
2   cloves garlic, minced or 2 tsp. minced garlic
1   Tbsp. olive or vegetable oil
½   cup apricot preserves
¼   cup barbecue sauce
¼   cup water
2   Tbsp. onion soup mix

Preheat oven to 375°. Cook the chicken in garlic and oil until brown. Place in an 8 inch baking dish. Combine everything else and pour over the chicken. Bake 25-30 minutes, uncovered, until the juices run clear. Serve over rice.

Chicken Alfredo

2   Tbsp. butter
1½   lbs. chicken breast, cubed
1   (16 oz.) pkg. penne pasta, cooked

Sauce

1   cup butter
1   clove garlic, crushed
1   cup heavy cream
1½   cups grated Parmesan cheese
     fresh parsley
½   tsp. salt
½   tsp. pepper
½   tsp. dried oregano
½   tsp. basil

In a pan over medium-high heat, melt butter. Add chicken breast.

Cook 8-10 minutes or until chicken is fully cooked. Remove from heat and set chicken aside.

In the same pan, over medium heat, melt butter for sauce and add the garlic. Cook until the garlic begins to soften. Add cream, Parmesan cheese and parsley to the garlic and butter, stirring until incorporated. Season with salt, pepper, oregano, and basil, and stir well to incorporate.

Add parmesan cheese and chicken and stir until cheese is melted. Pour over cooked penne pasta. Add parsley and extra parmesan if desired. Mix well.

Chicken Curry

1   lb. boneless skinless chicken breasts or thighs,
        cut into 1 inch pieces
2   tsp. curry powder
¼-1 tsp. cayenne pepper (optional, to taste)
¾   tsp. salt
¼   tsp. pepper
½   cup onion, chopped
1   Tbsp. canola oil
1   (13 oz.) can coconut milk
2   Tbsp. tomato paste
3   cups fresh baby spinach
1   cup tomato, chopped or 1 can died tomatoes
2   cups rice, cooked

Sprinkle chicken with curry, cayenne pepper, salt and pepper. In a large skillet, sauté chicken and onion in oil until chicken is no longer pink.

Stir in coconut milk and tomato paste. Bring to a boil. Reduce heat and simmer, uncovered, for 5 minutes or until thickened.

Add spinach and tomato. Cook 2-3 minutes longer or until spinach is wilted. Serve with rice.

- **Boneless, skinless chicken thighs can be cheaper than chicken breasts. In most recipes, they can be used interchangeably and have more flavor than chicken breasts.**

Mushroom Chicken

8   pieces chicken with skin
    all purpose flour (for coating)
2   cups water
1   tsp. chicken bouillon
1   bay leaf
1   tsp. onion salt
½-¾ cup mushrooms
¼   tsp. thyme
¾   cup heavy cream

Preheat oven to 350°. Place the chicken in a large ziptop bag with some flour and shake to coat the chicken in flour. Place in a greased 9x13 inch pan.

Mix the water, bouillon, bay leaf, onion salt and mushrooms and pour over the chicken. Cover with foil and bake 2 hours.

In the last 15 minutes, add the thyme and the heavy cream and continue baking with the foil off.

Chili Chicken

½   cup orange marmalade
2   Tbsp. chili powder
½   tsp. salt
8   chicken drumsticks

Preheat oven to 400°. Mix the first 3 ingredients in a zip lock bag. Add the chicken and coat. Place the chicken on a pan lined with foil that is well greased. Pour the extra marmalade mix over the chicken.

Bake 25-30 minutes or until done.

Easy Chicken Pot Pie

1⅔   cups frozen vegetables, thawed
1½   cups chicken or turkey, cooked and cubed
1   (10¾ oz.) can cream of chicken soup
¼   tsp. thyme
1   can refrigerator biscuits (8 biscuits)

Preheat oven to 400°. Combine everything but the biscuits in a greased 9 inch pie plate. Top with the biscuits. Bake 15-20 minutes, until biscuits are golden and veggies are tender. Serves 4-6.

Old Fashioned Chicken Pot Pie

You can make homemade biscuits to use in this recipe if you like.

1½   cups fresh mushrooms, sliced
1   cup fresh carrots, sliced
½   cup onions, chopped
⅓   cup butter or margarine
⅓   cup all purpose flour
1½   cups chicken broth
1½   cups milk
4   cups chicken, cooked and cubed
1   cup frozen peas
1   tsp. salt
1   can refrigerator biscuits

Preheat oven to 400°.

In a saucepan, sauté mushrooms, carrots and onions in butter. Sprinkle with the flour and gradually add the broth and milk. Blend. Bring to a boil and cook 2 minutes or until thickened.

Add chicken, peas and salt. Pour into a well greased 2½ quart baking dish. Top with biscuits. Bake, uncovered, 15-20 minutes, until biscuits are golden brown.

Crockpot Turkey

1   turkey (about 6 lbs.) or turkey breast
1   pkg. onion soup mix, or
          use these seasonings to your taste:
             onion powder
             garlic powder
             salt
             pepper
             Italian seasonings

Rub the inside of the crockpot with butter. Rub turkey with the soup mix or sprinkle with the seasonings. Cover and cook on high 1 hour. Then cook on low for about 7 hours. Don't add liquid. It will have enough juice.

Turkey Tips

Buy a small 10 lb. turkey instead of chicken and slow roast in a large crockpot.

You can add things like onions, carrots and celery to the bottom of the crockpot.

Use the leftovers for turkey enchiladas (in place of chicken), turkey sandwiches for lunch or on salads.

For quick dinners, wrap leftover turkey with some gravy in foil and freeze. Pull out of freezer and bake at 350° for 20-30 minutes, until warmed.

Can't find a small turkey? Some butchers will cut turkeys in half before you leave the store. Ask if they will do this if you can't find a smaller turkey.

Garlic Roast Pork

1	cup fresh cilantro, chopped
½	cup orange juice
½	cup lime juice
9	cloves garlic, minced or 3 Tbsp. minced garlic
3	Tbsp. oregano, finely chopped
1½	Tbsp. olive oil
	salt and pepper (to taste)
1	(5 lb.) boneless pork shoulder roast with fat cap
	lime wedges, for serving

In a large, resealable plastic bag, combine cilantro, orange and lime juices, garlic, oregano, olive oil, salt and pepper. Add the pork shoulder, seal the bag and turn to coat. Transfer the bag to a large baking dish and refrigerate the pork overnight, turning the bag once or twice.

Remove the pork from the marinade and scrape off the garlic and herbs. Discard the marinade. Season the pork all over with salt and pepper and transfer to a large casserole dish or pan. Let stand at room temperature for 1 hour.

Preheat the oven to 400°. Roast the pork, fat side up, for 1 hour, until lightly browned. Reduce the oven temperature to 300° and roast for 4 hours longer, until the pork is very tender and the fat cap is crispy. Let rest for 30 minutes. Chop the fat cap into bite-size pieces. Cut, shred or pull apart the pork and garnish with the crispy cap pieces. Serve with lime wedges.

Baked Pork Chops
And Potatoes

	vegetable oil
⅓	cup onions, chopped
6	pork chops
	salt and pepper (to taste)
4	cups potatoes, thickly sliced
1	(10¾ oz.) can cream of mushroom soup
1¼	cups milk

Preheat oven to 350°. Pour a couple of teaspoons of vegetable oil in pan. Add the onions and sauté. Add the pork chops. Season with salt and pepper. Brown on both sides.

Place the potatoes in a 2 quart greased baking dish and arrange the pork chops on top. Add the soup and milk to the cooked onions in the skillet. Stir and heat. Pour on top of the pork chops and potatoes.

Bake, covered, for 30 minutes. Uncover and bake 30-40 more minutes. Serves 6.

Pork Chop Dinner

4	pork chops (¾ inch thick)
2	Tbsp. cooking oil
4	medium potatoes, peeled and sliced
2	medium onions, sliced
2	medium carrots, sliced
2	Tbsp. butter or margarine
1	tsp. salt
1	tsp. pepper

Preheat oven to 350°. Brown the pork chops in oil in a skillet over medium-high heat. Place in a greased 9x13 inch baking pan. Layer the potatoes, onions and carrots over the pork chops. Dot with butter. Sprinkle with salt and pepper. Cover and bake 55-60 minutes or until the pork chops are done.

Slow Cooked Pork Ribs

1	rack of pork baby back ribs
	juice of one lemon
¼	cup dry rub
½	cup barbecue sauce

Preheat oven to 300°. Remove excess fat from ribs. Peel the silver skin off the back of the ribs - lift with a sharp knife and grab with a paper towel to remove. Cut ribs apart into individual pieces, if desired. Rub ribs all over with lemon juice. Coat ribs with dry rub. Place, meat side down, in a large baking pan, and cover tightly with foil, shiny side out. Bake in the oven for 2½ hours. Remove from oven and pour off liquid. Brush barbecue sauce over all sides of ribs.

Grill
To finish ribs on the grill, remove from the pan and place ribs on the grill basting and turning a few times for about 10 minutes.

Oven
To finish ribs in the oven, set oven to broil and return ribs to the same middle oven rack, uncovered. Baste and broil about 5 minutes per side, watching so they don't burn. They will be so tender, it's best to turn them using gloved hands. (If foil starts to burn, transfer ribs to a clean sheet of foil for broiling.)

A mother's patience is like a tube of toothpaste - it is never quite all gone.

Rib Dry Rub

¼   cup brown sugar, packed
2   tsp. chili powder
2   tsp. sweet paprika
1   tsp. salt
1   tsp. dry mustard
1   tsp. dried oregano
½   tsp. garlic powder
½   tsp. onion powder
¼   tsp. pepper

Combine everything.

Rib Barbecue Sauce

1   tsp. onion powder
1   tsp. garlic powder
½   cup cider vinegar
½   cup water
½   cup ketchup
½   cup brown sugar
2   Tbsp. molasses
2   Tbsp. spicy mustard
1   Tbsp. Worcestershire Sauce
2   tsp. chili powder (NOT powdered chili pepper)

Add everything to a saucepan over medium-high heat and bring to a boil.
Reduce heat and cook uncovered, stirring occasionally, for about
25 minutes. Sauce will thicken as it cools.

How To Make Casseroles

1   cup main ingredient
1   cup second ingredient
1-2 cups starchy ingredient
1½   cups binder
½   cup of "goodie"
      seasonings
      toppings

You can mix and match the ingredients any way you want, but use ingredients that go together. (See example on p.257)

For Example, Use:

Chicken, corn tortillas and enchilada sauce
Chicken, spinach, cream of mushroom soup and Parmesan cheese

Don't Use:

Turkey, enchilada sauce and Italian seasonings
Tuna, cumin and Worcestershire sauce

Mix ingredients of your choice. If your casserole ever seems too dry, just add ¼-½ cup cream, milk or stock.

When adding your toppings, try tossing the crackers, croutons or other toppings in some melted butter before sprinkling on top.

Preheat oven to 350°. Place in a greased, oven-proof dish. If most of your ingredients, like your veggies, are raw, bake about 30-45 minutes or until everything is tender.

If everything you use is already cooked, then bake at 350° for about 20 minutes, or until everything is warmed through.

When serving your warm casserole, top each serving with a dollop of sour cream or yogurt.

Here are some examples of each type of ingredient:

Main Ingredient

Tuna
Seafood
Chicken
Turkey
Ham
Roast beef
Hamburger

Second Ingredient

Mushrooms
Hard boiled eggs
Any canned, frozen or fresh
    vegetable (celery, carrots, peas,
    beans, broccoli, tomatoes, etc.)
Or additional 1 cup of the main
    ingredient

Starchy Ingredient

Rice
Noodles
Potatoes
Tortillas

Binder

Sour cream
Mayonnaise
Creamed soup (chicken, mushroom,
    celery)
Cream sauce (white sauce)
Tomato sauce or paste
Enchilada sauce
Cottage cheese

Goodies

Stuffed or ripe olives
Nuts, almonds or cashews
Water chestnuts
Pimentos
Green chiles
Cheese

Seasonings

Spices
Garlic, chopped
Onion, chopped
Green pepper, chopped
Worcestershire sauce
Lemon juice
Soy sauce

Toppings
Chinese noodles
Potato chips, crushed
Butter crackers (Ritz), crushed
Croutons
Cheese

Basic Casserole

3   cups turkey or chicken, cubed and cooked
3   medium carrots, cut into bite-size pieces
3   celery stalks, cut into bite-size pieces
3   red potatoes, cut into bite-size pieces
1   (10¾ oz.) can cream of chicken soup
½-¾ soup can of water
     salt and pepper (to taste)

Preheat oven to 350°. Place the turkey or chicken in a well greased 2 quart baking dish. Layer the veggies on top. Mix the soup, water and salt and pepper. Then pour over everything.

Bake 60 to 75 minutes, until tender. If you're using frozen veggies, cut the baking time in half. Makes 4-5 servings.

- **This casserole recipe is a great way to use your leftover turkey. You can use chicken, too. If you don't have much time, use frozen vegetables and cut down on the cooking time. If you're not using frozen potatoes, but the other vegetables are frozen, cook the potatoes first.**

- **It is nice to have extra casseroles in the freezer in case you need a quick meal. If you aren't sure a casserole will freeze well, make only one to eat that night. Then freeze just a few tablespoons of it to see how it works. If it works, then the next time you make it, you can make two - one to eat and one to freeze for a future meal.**

Vegetable Casserole

You don't need meat every night. Here's a good one dish vegetable meal.

1   (16 oz.) pkg. frozen broccoli, carrots and cauliflower mix,
        thawed and drained
1   (10¾ oz.) can cream of mushroom soup
⅓   cup sour cream
1   (2.8 oz.) can Durkee French fried onions
1½   cups cheese, shredded

Preheat oven to 350°. Combine everything except half of the cheese and fried onions. Pour into 1 quart greased baking dish.

Bake, covered, for 30 minutes. Top with remaining cheese and fried onions. Bake, uncovered, for 5 minutes.

Pizza Casserole

3   cups macaroni twists, uncooked
1   lb. ground beef or ground sausage
1   onion, chopped
1   green pepper, chopped
1   (4 oz.) can mushrooms
1   (32 oz.) jar spaghetti sauce
1   (10 oz.) can pizza sauce
4   oz. pepperoni
1   lb. mozzarella cheese, grated

Boil macaroni twists for 20 minutes. Brown ground beef, onion and pepper.

Preheat oven to 350°. Mix everything except cheese together in a greased 9x13 inch pan. Bake 45 minutes. Add cheese in the last 5 minutes.

Chow Mein Hot Dish

1	lb. ground beef
1	onion, chopped
2	cups celery, sliced
½	cup uncooked rice*
½	cup soy sauce
½	cup water
1	(4 oz.) can mushrooms
1	(10¾ oz.) can cream of mushroom soup
1	small can bean spouts
1	small can sliced water chestnuts
	Chinese noodles

Preheat oven to 375°. Brown ground beef and onions. Mix everything but Chinese noodles together (including liquid from mushrooms and bean sprouts) into ground beef. Place in a greased 9x9 inch pan.
Bake 1½ hours. Top with Chinese noodles.

To double: use a 9x13 inch pan.

* This recipe takes longer to cook because of the uncooked rice. You could use 1½ cups of cooked rice but, if you do, don't use the liquid from the mushrooms and bean sprouts. That will cut the cooking time in half.

• **Use Ramen noodles or instant rice in your casseroles. This makes preparation easier since you don't need to cook these before you add them to the dish.**

• **If you have time, roast your veggies before adding them to your casserole for some added flavor.**

Hamburger/Hot Dog Bar

Try having a hamburger/hot dog bar this year. Line up the "fixins" table with many different things. You can add as many or as few things as you like to your table or have all your guests bring 1-2 of their favorite unusual toppings.

Here are some items you might include:

- Monterey Jack cheese and sliced jalapenos
- Swiss cheese and mushrooms
- mozzarella, American, provolone cheese
- coleslaw
- tomatoes, peppers and onions
- avocado
- red, green or yellow peppers
- salsa and different relishes
- different pickles and olives
- bread and butter pickles
- garlic pickles
- different flavored mustards, mayo or sauces
- horseradish mustard or honey mustard
- Dijon mustard
- different barbecue sauces
- a variety of different buns and rolls

- **If you have a couple of extra bratwurst, hot dogs or hamburger patties, slice or crumble them and use them on top of homemade or frozen pizza.**

Spicy Fish

2	(6 oz.) fish fillets
¼	tsp. garlic powder
	salt and pepper (to taste)
¼	cup salsa
½	tsp. lime juice or juice from half a lime

Preheat oven to 350°. Place the fish on a greased (or foil lined) baking sheet. Sprinkle with garlic powder, salt and pepper. Pour on the salsa. Then top with the lime juice. Bake 15-20 minutes, until it flakes with a fork.

For other variations, use lemon pepper, a pat of butter, other fresh herbs or green onions.

Cajun Baked Catfish

Spicy, but not too spicy for those who like things mild

2	Tbsp. canola oil
2	Tbsp. garlic salt
2	tsp. thyme
2	tsp. paprika
½	tsp. cayenne pepper
½	tsp. hot pepper sauce
¼	tsp. pepper
4	(8 oz.) catfish fillets

Preheat oven to 450°. Combine the first 7 ingredients. Brush on the catfish. Place in a 9x13 inch pan sprayed with non stick spray. Bake 10-13 minutes or until the fish fillets are flaky.

If you have young children, you can use half the spices but if you are serving to adults who like it hot, you can double it.

Prefer a coating? Dip in egg and milk as usual and add these spices to the crumbs you use to dip the fillets in.

Baked Fish And Vegetables

4   fish fillets
4   medium potatoes, cut into 1 inch cubes
4   medium carrots, cut into 1 inch pieces
4   small onions, quartered
4   Tbsp. butter or margarine
     salt, pepper, garlic powder and celery seed (to taste)

Preheat oven to 350°. On each of four square 9 inch pieces of aluminum foil, place a fish fillet and a portion of potatoes, carrots and onions. Add 1 tablespoon of butter or margarine to each square. Sprinkle with the seasonings.

Fold the foil over and seal the edges well. Bake 45 minutes on a cookie sheet. This can also be put on the grill. Serves 4.

Fish Fillet Bundles

4   fresh or frozen fish fillets (6 oz. each), thawed
     grated Parmesan cheese
     cayenne pepper
2   medium zucchini, cut into ¼ inch slices
1   small sweet red pepper, sliced thin
     salt (to taste)

Place the fish on heavy foil and sprinkle with Parmesan cheese and cayenne pepper. Top with the zucchini and pepper. Salt to taste. Seal up in foil. Grill, covered, over indirect heat for about 8-10 minutes, until the fish is flaky.

Beans And Rice

1   Tbsp. bacon grease or canola oil
2   celery ribs, chopped (optional)
1   medium green pepper, chopped (optional)
1   medium onion, chopped
1   (28 oz.) can diced tomatoes, undrained
1   (16 oz.) can kidney beans, rinsed and drained
2   cups brown rice, cooked
2   tsp. Worcestershire sauce
1½ tsp. chili powder
¼   tsp. pepper
¼   cup Cheddar cheese, shredded
¼   cup sour cream
2   green onions, chopped

In a large nonstick skillet, heat oil over medium-high heat. Add celery, green pepper and onion. Cook and stir until tender.

Stir in tomatoes, beans, rice, Worcestershire sauce, chili powder and pepper. Bring to a boil. Reduce heat and simmer, covered, until heated through, about 7-9 minutes. Top with cheese, sour cream and green onions.

I love spending time with my BFF-bowl of fattening food.

Notes

Desserts

Dessert Tips

- **Prepare ahead of time for your baking.** Mix cookie dough as early as the day before, place in the refrigerator and bake the next day. The chilling improves the texture of the cookie when baked.

- **For fast bread crumbs or graham cracker crumbs,** place dried bread or graham crackers in a plastic bag and roll with a rolling pin.

- **If you make a lot of graham cracker pie crusts,** crush a large amount of graham crackers into crumbs in a food processor all at once. Store in a large airtight container with a scoop and you'll have them handy and ready whenever you need them.

- **Add peanut butter to chocolate sauce** and pour over vanilla or chocolate ice cream.

- **Do not wash fresh berries** until you're ready to use them.

- **Thin canned chocolate frosting with a little milk** and use it as a quick and easy dip for strawberries, bananas and other fruit.

- **To save on sugar when making fruit crisps, pies or cobblers,** try adding 1 teaspoon baking soda and using half the amount of sugar. The chemical reaction of the baking soda keeps them just as sweet. You may have to adjust it depending on the sweetness of the fruit.

- **When making pies, you may have to adjust the amount of sugar or thickening agent** (cornstarch, flour or tapioca) to the fruit you are using because some fruit can be sweeter or juicier. Just add a little less or a little more.

- **If you are out of food coloring,** try adding a spoonful of cherry or strawberry Jello (or whatever color you need) to your frosting to color it. This also makes it extra tasty.

Coconut Cake

1   (15 oz.) box yellow or white cake mix
1   (14 oz.) can sweetened condensed milk
1   (8 oz.) container whipped topping
1   (8 oz.) pkg. flaked coconut
1   (15 oz.) can crushed pineapple (optional)

Bake cake in a 9x13 inch pan according to box instructions. As soon as it comes out of the oven, pierce it with a fork and pour the can of milk over entire cake. Chill for at least 1 hour. Mix coconut (and pineapple, if desired) into whipped topping and spread over top of cake. Keep chilled until ready to use.

Grandma's Turtle Cake

1   (15 oz.) box German chocolate cake mix
      (plus ingredients on box to make cake)
¾   cup butter or margarine, softened
1   (14 oz.) pkg. Kraft caramels or caramel bits
½   cup evaporated milk
1   cup nuts
1   cup semi-sweet chocolate chips

Preheat oven to 375°. Prepare cake as directed on box. Add softened butter and pour half of the mixture into a 9x13 inch greased pan. Bake 10 minutes. While the cake is baking, melt together caramels and milk. Pour melted caramels on partially baked cake, sprinkle with nuts and chocolate chips. Pour remaining batter on top. Bake 25-30 minutes more.

- **If your coconut becomes dry, just sprinkle it with a little milk and let it sit for 10 minutes.**

Carrot Cake

2   cups sugar
2   (4 oz.) jars strained carrot baby food*
4   eggs
1½   cups vegetable oil
1½   tsp. baking soda
½   tsp. salt
2   tsp.cinnamon
2   cups all purpose flour

Preheat oven to 325°. Grease and flour 3 (8 or 9 inch) cake pans.

Mix together sugar, baby food, eggs and vegetable oil. Add baking soda, salt and cinnamon. Mix. Add flour and blend well with mixer for about 2 minutes.

Pour batter into prepared pans. Bake 25-30 minutes, or until golden brown. Cool completely.

*If you like the taste of shredded carrots in your carrot cake, use 4 oz. baby food and ½ cup shredded carrots.

*½ cup of cooked mashed carrots can be used in place of baby food.

Cream Cheese Frosting

½   cup butter, softened
1   (8 oz.) pkg. cream cheese, softened
1   lb. powdered sugar
1   tsp. vanilla

Mix all ingredients with handheld electric mixer and blend until smooth and creamy. Frost layers, top, and sides of cooled cake.

Boston Cream Cake

1   (15 oz.) yellow cake mix
2   (3 oz.) boxes vanilla pudding
4   cups milk
1   can chocolate frosting

Bake cake in a 9x13 inch pan according to box instructions. When cake is done, poke holes in it with something like the handle of a wooden spoon. While it is cooling, mix pudding mix and milk. Pour immediately over cake. Chill.

When cake is chilled, microwave frosting for a few seconds to soften and pour over cake.

Apple Spice Cake

1   (15 oz.) pkg. spice cake mix
1   (21 oz.) can apple pie filling
2   eggs
2   Tbsp. vegetable oil
    nuts

Preheat oven to 350°. Mix everything at medium speed for 2 minutes. Pour into a well greased 9x13 inch baking pan and bake 30-35 minutes or until a toothpick comes out clean when inserted into it. Frost with caramel frosting (p. 277) or top with caramel ice cream topping.

- **If you often make cakes from scratch, when you are making your next cake, make your own mix while you have all the ingredients out. Just measure all the dry ingredients into plastic bags and store 2-3 bags on a shelf. Then, the next time you make a cake, all you have to add is your wet ingredients. You could also do this with muffins, quick breads or even cookies.**

Dump Cake

1   (20 oz.) can crushed pineapple
1   (21 oz.) can cherry pie filling
1   (21 oz.) can apple pie filling
1   (15 oz.) pkg. yellow cake mix
½   cup nuts, chopped
½   cup butter or margarine, cut into 16-20 slices

Preheat oven to 350°. Grease a 9x13 inch cake pan. Dump in the undrained pineapple and spread over entire pan. Do the same with the pie fillings. Next, dump the cake mix and spread evenly. Sprinkle nuts on top. Place the butter or margarine on top of everything in a single layer so as much of the cake mix as possible is covered. DO NOT MIX. Bake 1 hour or until golden on top.

Variations

- You can use lemon, strawberry or spice cake mixes.

- You could also replace the 2 cans of pie filling with 1 can blueberry pie filling, 1 cup coconut and 1 cup pecans.

- **I use a lot of recipes that call for drained pineapple, so I always have a couple ounces of juice that I hate to throw away. Save the juice in a container in the freezer and when you need some juice for a recipe, you have it.**

Pineapple
Upside Down Cake

¼   cup butter
1   cup brown sugar, packed
1   (20 oz.) can pineapple slices, drained, juice reserved
1   (6 oz.) jar maraschino cherries without stems, drained
1   box yellow cake mix
      plus ingredients to make cake

Heat oven to 350°. In a 9x13 inch baking pan, melt butter in the oven. Sprinkle brown sugar evenly over butter. Arrange pineapple slices on brown sugar. Place a cherry in the center of each pineapple slice and arrange remaining cherries around slices. Press everything gently into the brown sugar.

Add enough water to reserved pineapple juice to measure 1 cup. Make cake batter as directed on box, substituting pineapple juice mixture for the water. Pour batter over pineapple and cherries.

Bake 42 to 48 minutes or until a toothpick inserted in the center comes out clean.

Immediately run a knife around the side of the pan to loosen cake. Place a serving plate upside down onto the pan. Turn the plate and pan over. *pla* Leave pan over cake 5 minutes so brown sugar topping can drizzle over cake. Remove pan. Cool 30 minutes. Serve warm or cool. Store, covered, in the refrigerator.

*   Blot
     Cherries
        + Pineapple Slices

Round pan.

274

Rhubarb Cake

½   cup butter or margarine
1½   cups sugar
1   egg
1   cup buttermilk
1   tsp. vanilla
1   tsp. baking soda
½   tsp. salt
2½   cups all purpose flour
3   cups rhubarb, diced

Preheat oven to 350°. Mix all ingredients. Add the rhubarb last. Pour into a well-greased 9x13 inch pan. Sprinkle with 1 cup brown sugar and ½ cup nuts. Bake 55 minutes.

Never Fail Fruitcake

This is a big fruitcake recipe but you can easily half it. Using half, you can make 22 cupcakes but if you do, only bake them for 40 minutes.

1   lb. candied cherries, chopped
1   lb. dates, pitted and chopped
1   lb. candied pineapple, chopped
1   lb. pecans, chopped
4   (8 oz.) pkgs. coconut
3   Tbsp. all purpose flour
2   (14 oz.) cans sweetened condensed milk

Preheat oven to 300°. Grease two 9x5 inch loaf pans and line with brown paper or parchment paper. Mix everything very well and press into pans. Bake 1½ hours. Cool and remove from pan.

• **If you freeze strawberries, rhubarb or anything like that, pre-measure them before freezing in the amounts you usually need for your favorite recipes. Be sure to label the bag.**

Caramel Frosting

½   cup butter or margarine
1   cup brown sugar, packed
¼   cup milk
2   cups powdered sugar

Heat butter or margarine over medium heat in a 2 quart saucepan. When butter or margarine is melted, stir in brown sugar. Heat to boiling, stirring constantly. Reduce heat to low and boil 2 minutes longer, still stirring. Stir in milk and heat to boiling.

Remove from heat and cool. Slowly stir in powdered sugar. Place the saucepan of frosting in a bowl of very cold water and beat the frosting until smooth. If the frosting is too stiff, add an additional 1 teaspoon of milk at a time until the frosting is smooth. Frosts one 9x13 inch cake.

Chocolate Ganache

8   oz. bittersweet chocolate chips or
        chocolate chopped into roughly even pieces
½   cup butter, cut into small pieces

Place the chocolate in a microwave safe bowl. Microwave, stirring every 20 seconds until mostly melted. Add the butter and stir. Use immediately.

Vanilla Glaze

4   Tbsp. butter, melted
1   tsp. vanilla
3   cups powdered sugar
     milk, enough to make a thin icing (about ½ cup)

Mix together and add enough milk to make a thin glaze.

For lemon glaze: Add 1 tsp. lemon juice to vanilla glaze.

Cake Mix Cookies

1   pkg. cake mix (any flavor)
½   cup oil
2   eggs, slightly beaten

Preheat oven to 350°. In large bowl, combine all ingredients. Blend well. Drop dough by rounded teaspoonfuls 2 inches apart onto ungreased cookie sheets. Bake 10-15 minutes or until set. Cool 1 minute. Remove from cookie sheets.

Note: Different cake mixes will act differently. Yellow cake mix spreads out more than the other mixes. See suggested variations below.

High Altitude: Add 2 Tbsp. flour and bake as usual.

Variations

Fluffy, Chewy Cookies: Add ½ cup flour.

Sugar Cookies: Yellow cake mix. Add 1 tsp vanilla.

Chocolate Chip Cookies: Yellow cake mix. Add 1 cup chocolate chips.

Double Chocolate Cookies: Devil's food chocolate cake mix. Add 1 cup semi-sweet or dark chocolate chips.

Oatmeal Chocolate Chip Cookies: Yellow or white cake mix. Add ½ cup quick cooking oatmeal and 1 cup chocolate chips.

Oatmeal Raisin Cookies: Yellow cake mix. Add ½ cup rolled oats and ½ cup raisins.

Chocolate Oatmeal Raisin Cookies: Devil's food chocolate cake mix. Add 1 cup semi-sweet chocolate chips, ½ cup rolled oats and ½ cup raisins.

German Chocolate Cookies: German chocolate cake mix. Add 1 cup caramel bits, ½ cup pecans and ½ cup coconut.

Chocolate Caramel Cookies: German chocolate cake mix. Add 1 cup caramel bits.

Black and White Cookies: Devil's food chocolate cake mix. Add 1 cup white chocolate chips.

Birthday Cake Cookies: White cake mix. Add ½ cup sprinkles.

Rocky Road Cookies: Devil's food chocolate cake mix. Add ½ cup marshmallows and 1 cup chopped almonds.

Chocolate Peanut Butter Cookies: Devil's food chocolate cake mix. Add 1 cup peanut butter chips.

Chocolate Strawberry Cookies: Strawberry cake mix. Add ½ cup chocolate chips

Red Velvet Cookies: Red velvet cake. Add 1 cup white chocolate chips.

Cinnamon Spice Cookies: Spice Cake. Add 1 cup cinnamon chips.

Carrot Cake Cookies: Carrot cake. Add 1 cup white chocolate chips.

Lemon Cookies: Lemon cake mix. Add 1 cup white chocolate chips.

Butter Pecan Cookies: Butter pecan cake mix. Add 1 cup butterscotch chips.

Chocolate Mint Cookies: Devil's food chocolate cake mix. Add 1 cup Andes mint chips.

M&M Cookies: White chocolate cake mix. Add 1 cup M&M's.

Toffee Cookies: Yellow cake mix. Add 1 cup toffee chips.

Chocolate Cherry Cookies: Devil's food or dark chocolate cake mix. Add ½ cup chopped candied cherries and ½ cup dark chocolate chips.

S'mores: Chocolate cake mix. Add: ¾ cup marshmallow and ¾ cup graham crackers, crushed.

Snickerdoodle: White cake mix. Add 1 Tbsp. cinnamon. Make balls and roll in cinnamon and sugar. Then bake.

Cake Mix Cookies
(continued)

Banana Split Cookies: White or yellow cake mix. Add 1 small box banana pudding, ½ cup chocolate chips and ½ cup maraschino cherries, chopped.

Dreamsicle Cookies: Orange cake mix. Add 1 cup white chocolate chips.

Cherry Chip Cookies: Cherry Chip Cake Mix. Add 1 cup chocolate chips.

Tutti Frutti: Yellow Cake Mix. Add 1 cup Fruity Pebbles.

Double Cookie Cookies: Devil's food chocolate cake mix. Add ½ cup Oreos, crushed and ½ cup chocolate chips.

Cherry Delight: White cake mix. Add ½ cup dried cherries, ½ cup pecans, 1 Tbsp. fresh orange zest and ½ tsp. vanilla.

Raisin Spice Cookies: Spice Cake. Add 1 cup raisins.

Pumpkin Spice Cookies: Pumpkin cake mix. Add 1 cup pecans.

I ate healthy and exercised today so I had better wake up skinny in the morning.

Double Chocolate Cookies

1   (10-12 oz.) bag semi-sweet chocolate chips
¼   cup butter
¾   cup brown sugar
2   eggs
1   tsp. vanilla
½   tsp. baking powder
½   tsp. salt
⅔   cup all purpose flour

Preheat oven to 350°. Melt 1½ cups chocolate chips (¾ of the bag) and butter together. Add remaining ingredients in the order listed, including the remaining chocolate chips in bag. Drop by teaspoonfuls on greased cookie sheet.

Bake 12-15 minutes. Rotate halfway through baking. (Turn the pan around.).

- **When baking cookies, we often overbake them, which makes them hard and crunchy. If you want a soft cookie, watch the time and *almost* undercook them. If you are given a cooking time like 10-15 minutes, use the 10 minutes.**

- **Keep a plastic knife in your canisters to level off things like flour or sugar.**

- **When spraying pans with cooking spray or when flouring them, hold the pans over the sink. Then the over-spray will go into the sink and you will avoid a mess.**

Oatmeal Apple Cookies

1   cup butter, softened
1   cup brown sugar, packed
½   cup sugar
2   eggs
1   tsp. vanilla
1½   cups all purpose flour
2   tsp. cinnamon
1   tsp. baking soda
3   cups old fashioned oats
½   cup dried apples, chopped

Preheat oven to 350°. Cream butter and sugars. Add eggs and vanilla. Combine flour, cinnamon and baking soda and add to butter mixture. Fold in oats and apples.

Drop by rounded tablespoonful onto an ungreased cookie sheet, 2 inches apart. Bake 10-12 minutes. Let stand 1 minute before removing from the cookie sheet.

Double Chocolate Peanut Butter Cookies

1   cup chunky peanut butter
2   Tbsp. vegetable oil
2   eggs
1   pkg. fudge brownie mix (9x13 inch pan size), not baked
½   cup water
½   cup unsalted peanuts
1   (12 oz.) pkg. semi-sweet chocolate chips or milk chocolate
           candy bars, coarsely chopped

Preheat oven to 350°. Cream peanut butter and oil. Beat in eggs. Stir in brownie mix and water. Fold in peanuts and chocolate. Drop by heaping tablespoons onto a greased baking sheet, 2 inches apart.

Bake 12-14 minutes or until lightly brown.

3 Ingredient Peanut Butter Cookies

1   cup peanut butter
1   cup sugar
1   egg

Preheat oven to 350°. Combine the peanut butter, sugar and egg. Mix until smooth. Drop spoonfuls of dough onto a greased or lined baking sheet. Bake 6-8 minutes. Do not overbake! These cookies are best when they are still soft and just barely brown on the bottoms.

Peanut Butter Kiss Cookies

Add a chocolate kiss to the top of each cookie immediately after baking.

- **Use shiny cookie sheets and not dark or burned ones. In the same way that dark clothes and car upholstery absorb heat, dark baking sheets cause cookies to burn more easily. If you only have a dark baking pan, turn down your temperature 25°.**

- **If you prefer chewy cookies, bake them only until the edges are golden brown. The centers will look a little underbaked. You will need to let them cool for a minute or two before removing from the pan.**

- **If you have a small amount of dough to bake or if you don't have a cookie sheet, turn over a regular baking pan (like a 9x13 or 9x9 inch) and bake your items on the bottom.**

Chocolate Whoopie Pies

½   cup sugar
¼   cup shortening
½   cup dark corn syrup
1   egg
½   cup cocoa
½   cup sour milk
½   tsp. baking soda
1   tsp. salt
1   tsp. vanilla
2   cups all purpose flour
    nuts (optional)

Preheat oven to 350°. Mix all the ingredients together in a bowl. Using a ¼ cup ice cream scoop, drop onto a greased cookie sheet. Bake 5-10 minutes.

When cool, mix filling and spread on half of the cookies. Then top with the other halves.

Filling

2¾   cups powdered sugar
¼   cup half and half
¼   tsp. salt

Variations

- **Mint Chocolate:** Add ¼ tsp. peppermint extract and a few drops green food coloring in the filling.

- **Marshmallow:** Use marshmallow creme for filling.

- **Peanut Butter:** Add 2 Tbsp. peanut butter to filling.

- **Chocolate:** Add 1-2 Tbsp. baking cocoa to filling.

- **Cherry:** Add 1 Tbsp. cherry gelatin powder to filling.

- **Strawberry:** Add 1 Tbsp. strawberry gelatin powder to filling.

- **Cheesecake:** Add 3 Tbsp. cream cheese to filling.

Rocky Road Brownies

1   pan brownies, baked
     mini marshmallows
     nuts, coarsely chopped
1   cup semi-sweet chocolate chips
3   Tbsp. butter or margarine

Bake your favorite brownie recipe. While still hot, sprinkle with mini marshmallows and coarsely chopped peanuts or nuts. Melt chocolate chips and butter or margarine together and spread or drizzle over the marshmallows.

- **If you want your brownies to be picture perfect for a special occasion, here are a few ways to accomplish that:**

  - **Line your pan with foil before you bake so you can just lift the brownies out.**

  - **Use a ruler and cut off the outer edges, saving the scraps for snacking or crumbling on top of ice cream.**

  - **Use a ruler to score the cutting lines. Cut them with a straight downward motion, not sawing.**

  - **If you are cutting brownies with frosting, wipe off the knife between each cut.**

  - **Use a plastic knife to cut brownies without tearing.**

Rice Krispie Treats

¾   cup butter or margarine
2   (10 oz.) bags mini marshmallows
½   tsp. vanilla
     pinch salt
9   cups Rice Krispies cereal

Lightly grease a 9×13 inch baking pan. Melt butter over medium heat in a separate large pan. Once melted, add marshmallows. Stir until the marshmallows are melted.

Remove from heat. Stir in vanilla and salt. Fold in cereal, coating well. Lightly grease a spatula and spread the mixture into the baking pan. Lightly press down until mixture is even in the pan. Let cool 1 hour.

Cut into squares with a greased knife. To store, place in layers between greased sheets of parchment or wax paper.

Variations

- **Coconut:** Add 1½ cups shredded coconut.

- **Peanut Butter Cup:** Add a couple tablespoons of peanut butter after marshmallows are melted.

- **Rocky Road:** Add mini marshmallows, walnuts or almonds and chocolate chips after marshmallows are melted.

- **Rainbow:** Use Fruity Pebbles cereal instead of Rice Krispies.

- **Mint Chip:** Add ½ tsp. mint extract and a few drops of green food coloring into marshmallows. Top with chocolate.

- **Candy:** Add Reese's Pieces, M&M's, Twix, Rolos, Skittles or any of your favorite candies after marshmallows are melted or just press on top.

- **Oreo:** Break up some Oreo cookies and add to the mixture after marshmallows are melted. Leave a few to press into the top.

Holiday Rice Krispie Treats

Add food coloring to the melted marshmallows to match the holiday. Then, using a large cookie cutter (stars, pumpkins, hearts, Christmas trees), cut them into holiday shapes.

Rice Krispie Pops

Roll Rice Krispie treats into balls and stick a popsicle stick into each one. Then, roll them in:

- sprinkles
- candies, chopped
- mini chocolate chips
- coconut
- melted chocolate
- nuts

Make a decision - right or wrong, decide. The world is full of flat squirrels who couldn't decide which way they were going.

Chocolate Cherry Rice Krispie Treats

6   Tbsp. butter
1½   Tbsp. cherry gelatin powder*
1   (16 oz.) pkg. mini marshmallows
8   cups Rice Krispies cereal
1½   cups dark chocolate chips, melted

Melt butter, gelatin powder and marshmallows in a large pan over low heat. Stir constantly.

When marshmallows are melted, fold in cereal. Then press mixture** into a 9×13 inch pan or baking sheet. Frost or drizzle with melted chocolate. Set for 1 hour. Store in an airtight container.

* You could use strawberry gelatin in place of the cherry.

**To make it easier to press them into the pan, put a little bit of butter or spray your fingertips with a small amount of cooking spray and then press them into the pan. This will keep the marshmallow from sticking to your fingers and get the job done quickly and cleanly!

My therapist told me the way to achieve true inner peace is to finish what you start. So far I have finished 2 bags of M & M's and a piece of chocolate cake. I feel better already.

Brownie Marshmallow Bars

1   pkg. fudge brownie mix
1   (10½ oz.) pkg. mini marshmallows
2   cups semi-sweet chocolate chips
1   cup peanut butter
1   Tbsp. butter or margarine
1½   cups Rice Krispies cereal

Preheat oven to 350°. Mix brownies according to the package directions for fudge-like brownies and pour into a greased 9x13 inch pan.

Bake 28-30 minutes. Top with marshmallows and bake 3 minutes more. The marshmallows will not be completely melted. Cool.

Melt chocolate chips, peanut butter and butter or margarine. Stir until smooth. Remove from heat. Add Rice Krispies cereal. Spread on brownies. Chill 1-2 hours before cutting.

Chocolate comes from cocoa,
which is a tree, which is a plant,
so that makes chocolate a salad.

Easy Pumpkin Bars

⅓   cup sugar
⅓   cup oil
1   (15 oz.) can pumpkin
3   eggs
1   (15 oz.) yellow cake mix
3   tsp. pumpkin pie spice*
½   cup walnuts or pecans (optional)
1   can vanilla frosting
3   oz. cream cheese, softened

Preheat oven to 350°. Grease and flour a 15x10x1 inch jelly roll pan. Combine sugar, oil, pumpkin and eggs. Beat on high for 1 minute. Add cake mix and pumpkin pie spice. Mix 2 minutes on high speed. Fold in nuts, if desired.

Pour into the pan and bake 25-35 minutes or until a toothpick inserted in the center comes out clean.

Combine the frosting and cream cheese until smooth. Frost cooled bars. Store in the refrigerator.

*Pumpkin Pie Spice

1½   tsp. cinnamon
½   tsp. ginger
½   tsp. nutmeg
¼   tsp. allspice
¼   tsp. cloves

Mix and store in a spice bottle.

Toll House® Chocolate Chip Bars

1   cup butter, softened
¾   cup sugar
¾   cup brown sugar, packed
1   tsp. vanilla
2   eggs
2¼   cups all purpose flour
1   tsp. baking soda
1   tsp. salt
1   (12 oz.) pkg. semi-sweet chocolate chips
1   cup chopped nuts (optional)

Preheat oven to 375°. Grease a 15x10x1 inch jelly roll pan. Beat butter, both sugars and vanilla in a large mixing bowl. Add eggs one at a time, beating well after each.

Add flour, baking soda and salt. Gradually beat flour mixture into butter mixture.

Stir in chocolate chips and nuts. Spread into prepared pan.

Bake 20-25 minutes or until golden brown.

• **Store your cooking oil in a plastic squeeze bottle like the kind used for ketchup. Then you won't have to stop to unscrew the cap in the middle of making a recipe and it's easier not to use as much.**

Pie Filling

Many recipes call for canned pie filling, which is so convenient, but it can be expensive. If you can get free or very inexpensive fruit, it pays to make your own pie filling.

2	Tbsp. butter
1	tsp. cinnamon
2	cups fruit (peaches, apples, plums, blueberries, peeled, cored and cut)
⅓	cup sugar
3	Tbsp. water
1	Tbsp. + 1 tsp. cornstarch
2	Tbsp. water

Melt butter and cinnamon over medium heat. Stir in fruit, sugar and water. Cover and cook, stirring occasionally, for 4-6 minutes or until the fruit is very slightly softened.

In a small dish, combine cornstarch and 2 tablespoons water. Add to pan while stirring and continue to cook until fruit is soft (not mushy) and filling is thickened. Let bubble 1 minute. Cool.

If your pies are too runny, add 1 tablespoon of tapioca or cornstarch to your filling.

Trail Mix?

You mean M&M's with obstacles?

Blueberry Cream Pie

1	cup (8 oz.) sour cream
2	Tbsp. all purpose flour
¾	cup sugar
1	tsp. vanilla
¼	tsp. salt
1	egg, beaten
2½	cups blueberries, fresh, frozen or canned
1	(9 inch) pie crust, unbaked

Topping

1½	Tbsp. butter
3	Tbsp. walnuts or pecans, chopped
3	Tbsp. all purpose flour

Preheat oven to 400°. Combine the first 6 ingredients and beat on medium speed 5 minutes or until smooth. Fold in the blueberries and pour into the crust. Bake 25 minutes.

Combine the topping ingredients and sprinkle over the pie. Bake 10 more minutes. Chill and store in the refrigerator.

Ok, it has been 12 years now...
I'm beginning to think I'm not bloated.

Blueberry Pie

¾   cup sugar
4   Tbsp. cornstarch
¼   tsp. salt
½   tsp. cinnamon
1   tsp. lemon juice
4   cups blueberries
2   (9 inch) pie crusts, unbaked
1   Tbsp. butter

Preheat oven to 375°. Mix sugar, cornstarch, salt, cinnamon and lemon juice. Sprinkle over blueberries.

Line pie dish with one pie crust. Pour berry mixture into the crust, and dot with butter. Roll out second pie crust pastry and place on top. Crimp and flute edges.

Bake pie on lower shelf of oven for about 50 minutes or until the crust is golden brown.

If edges start to brown too much, place foil strips around edges of pie to keep from burning.

I may look like I'm deep in thought but 99% of the time I'm thinking about what I'm going to eat later.

Best Ever Chocolate Pie

2   (4 oz.) Hershey's candy bars with almonds
1½   cups heavy cream
20   large marshmallows (10 oz. bag)
1   graham cracker crust
      whipped topping or whipped cream

Break Hershey's bars and place into pan. Add 1 cup heavy cream and marshmallows. Stir continuously until melted. Remove from heat and add the rest of the heavy cream. Mix well. Pour into the pie crust. Refrigerate for 24 hours to set. Cover with whipped topping.

Chocolate Pecan Pie

1   (9 inch) pie crust, unbaked
1   cup semi-sweet chocolate chips
⅔   cup evaporated milk
2   Tbsp. butter
2   eggs, beaten slightly
1   cup sugar
2   Tbsp. all purpose flour
¼   tsp. salt
1   tsp. vanilla
1   cup pecans, chopped

Preheat oven to 375°. Heat chocolate chips, evaporated milk and butter until melted and creamy. Add all the remaining ingredients and mix. Pour into the pie crust. Bake 40 minutes.

• **Cover edges of pies with strips of foil if they seem to be browning too fast.**

Pecan Pie Tarts

Crust

½   cup sugar
¼   cup butter, softened
1   (3 oz.) pkg. cream cheese, softened
1   large egg
1¾   cups all purpose flour

Mix sugar, butter and cream cheese until smooth. Add egg and flour. Mix. Dough will be sticky. Cover and chill 1 hour.

Filling

⅓   cup light corn syrup
⅓   cup dark corn syrup
½   cup sugar
2   Tbsp. butter, melted
2   large eggs
1   tsp. vanilla
¾   cup pecans

Roll chilled dough into 1 inch balls. Press into the bottom and ⅔ of the way up the sides of each muffin space in a mini muffin tin.

Preheat oven to 350°. Mix filling ingredients except pecans and spoon into crusts. Top with pecans.

Bake 18-20 minutes or until lightly brown. Makes 3 dozen pecan pie tarts.

Chocolate Peanut Butter Pie

Crust
(You can use 2 store bought crusts if you prefer.)

20   Oreo cookies, crushed
¼   cup butter or margarine

Mix ingredients and press into a 9x13 inch pan.

Filling

1   (8 oz.) pkg. cream cheese, softened
¾   cup peanut butter
1½   cups powdered sugar
1   (8 oz.) container whipped topping

Beat cream cheese, peanut butter, and powdered sugar. Fold in whipped topping. Spread on crust. Chill at least 3 hours. You can freeze, but thaw before serving.

Variations

• You can add less peanut butter if the flavor is overpowering.

• Add chopped peanuts or walnuts.

• Drizzle with chocolate ice cream topping.

• Leave out the peanut butter altogether and add a couple tablespoons of cocoa. Then serve with fresh fruit like strawberries, raspberries or bananas.

• Add chocolate chips along with the peanut butter.

• Leave out the peanut butter and just use chocolate chips, sprinkles or crushed candies.

• Use a graham cracker crust for a less rich dessert.

Cheesecake

Graham Cracker Crust
(can use store bought)

1½   cups graham cracker crumbs
3   Tbsp. butter, melted
2   Tbsp. sugar

Preheat oven to 350°. Mix all ingredients and press into a 9 inch pie pan.
Bake 10 minutes.

Filling

4   (8 oz.) pkgs. cream cheese
¼   cup cornstarch
1⅔   cups sugar
1   Tbsp. vanilla
¾   cup whipping cream
3   eggs

Reduce oven to 300°. Beat everything but the eggs. Beat in eggs one at a
time. Pour into crust and bake 1 hour or until firm. Chill 3 hours.

No Bake Cheesecake

2   (8 oz.) pkgs. cream cheese (not lowfat)
1   (14 oz.) can sweetened condensed milk (not lowfat)
1   tsp. vanilla
¼   cup lemon juice
     graham cracker crust
     pie filling of your choice (for topping, optional)

Beat first 4 ingredients together. Spoon into a graham cracker crust. Chill.
Top with pie filling, if desired.

Chocolate Cheesecake

1   cup crushed chocolate wafer crumbs*
          (Nabisco Famous Chocolate Wafers)
3   Tbsp. sugar
3   Tbsp. butter, melted

Filling

2   cups semi-sweet chocolate chips
2   (8 oz.) pkgs. cream cheese, softened
¾   cup sugar
2   Tbsp. all purpose flour
2   large eggs, lightly beaten
1   tsp. vanilla
      strawberries and white chocolate shavings (optional)

Combine cookie crumbs, sugar and butter. Press into the bottom of a greased 9 inch springform pan or deep dish pie pan. Set aside.

Melt chocolate chips in the microwave, stirring until smooth. Set aside.

Preheat oven to 350°. In a large bowl, beat the cream cheese, sugar and flour until smooth. Add eggs and beat on low, just until combined. Stir in vanilla and melted chocolate, just until blended. Pour filling over crust.

Bake 40-45 minutes or until center is almost set. Cool on a wire rack for 10 minutes. Carefully run a knife around edge of pan to loosen.

Cool 1 hour longer. Refrigerate overnight.

Garnish slices with strawberries and chocolate shavings, if desired. Refrigerate leftovers.

*These can sometimes be hard to find. You can use graham crackers instead.

Cherry Cobbler

1   (15 oz.) yellow cake mix
2   (20 oz.) cans cherry pie filling*
½   cup (1 stick) butter or margarine, cold

Preheat oven to 350°. Pour cherry pie filling into a greased 9x13 inch pan. Sprinkle dry cake mix on top of pie filling. Cut butter into 16-20 slivers. Lay on top of dry cake mix as close as possible without overlapping, but it won't cover the entire top.

Bake 45-50 minutes.

*You may use any fruit pie filling you like.

Mike: Test with a fork and a cup of coffee. ;-) This was super delish!!

> The more you weigh, the harder it is to kidnap you. Stay safe - Eat cake.

Pumpkin Fluff

Crust

½   cup butter or margarine
1   cup all purpose flour
1   cup walnuts or pecans, chopped

Preheat oven to 325°. Mix ingredients and press into a 9x13 inch pan. Bake 20 minutes. Cool.

Filling

1   small (15 oz.) can pumpkin
1   (14 oz.) can sweetened condensed milk
1   (6 oz.) pkg. vanilla pudding
1½   tsp. pumpkin spice
1   (24 oz.) container whipped topping, divided

Mix the filling ingredients, reserving half of the whipped topping and spread on the cooled crust. Cover with the rest of the whipped topping. Refrigerate until ready to serve.

Pumpkin Crunch

1   (15 oz.) can solid pack pumpkin
1   (12 oz.) can evaporated milk
3   large eggs
1½   cups sugar
1   tsp. cinnamon
1   tsp. salt
1   (15 oz.) pkg. yellow cake mix
½   cup nuts
1   cup butter, melted

Preheat oven to 350°. Mix the pumpkin, milk, eggs, sugar, cinnamon and salt in a large bowl. Pour into a greased 9x13 inch pan. Sprinkle the dry cake mix over the pumpkin mixture. Sprinkle with nuts and drizzle with butter. Bake 50-55 minutes or until golden brown. Cool. Serve chilled with whipped topping.

2 Ingredient Pineapple Whip

1   whole pineapple - cut up and frozen overnight*
1   cup coconut milk (or milk of your choice)

Combine ingredients and blend in a blender or food processor, stirring as needed, until creamy. Makes about 3-4 servings.

Place leftover pineapple whip in an 8x8 inch pan and freeze in one layer.

*You may use canned pineapple.

Yogurt Whips

¾   cup plain Greek yogurt
¼   cup whipping cream
2   Tbsp. sugar
½   tsp. vanilla
      berries for topping (optional)
      mint leaves for garnish

Add all of the ingredients to a bowl except mint. Beat the ingredients together, starting on low and increasing the speed to high. Beat for several minutes or until the mixture is smooth and creamy, scraping down the sides of the bowl as needed.

Divide the yogurt into 4 small bowls, glasses or jars. Top each with berries and garnish with mint, if desired. Then serve.

- **If you have a small amount of whipped topping left over, place dollops of it on a piece of wax paper and freeze. Then place in an airtight container. When you need a quick topping for a dessert or something to go on a late night cup of hot cocoa, you can just grab one of these out of the freezer.**

2 Ingredient Ice Cream

2   cups heavy cream, very cold
1   (14 oz.) can sweetened condensed milk
2   tsp. vanilla (optional)

Mix cream on high speed until it becomes stiff, about 2-4 minutes. Fold in sweetened condensed milk. If you are adding in any of the optional extras, do that now. Transfer to a container with a lid and freeze for 6 hours.

Add-ins

- ¼ cup semi-sweet chocolate chips, chopped
- 2 Tbsp. chocolate syrup
- ¼ cup nuts
- ¼ cup maraschino cherries
- ¼ cup fruit, chopped
- ¼ cup cookies, crushed

Banana Ice Cream

4   bananas, very ripe, sliced and frozen

Blend the bananas in a blender or food processor until smooth. This may take a bit so just scrape down the blender as needed and keep blending.

Variations

- 2 Tbsp. chopped chocolate chips
- ½ cup strawberries
- ½ cup raspberries
- 2 Tbsp. peanut butter and chocolate syrup
- ½ cup cherries and ½ tsp. vanilla

Old Fashioned Ice Cream

2   cups heavy whipping cream
2   cups half and half or milk
1   cup sugar
2   tsp. vanilla

Combine all ingredients, stirring to dissolve sugar completely. Fill cylinder of ice cream maker no more than ⅔ full. Freeze according to ice cream maker directions. (Refrigerate any remaining mixture until ready to freeze.) Serve immediately or store in covered containers in freezer.

Variations

• **Raspberry or strawberry ice cream:** Substitute 2 cups fresh or frozen berries for 1 cup half and half. Puree berries in a blender or food processor. Stir into the other ingredients before freezing.

• **Chocolate chip ice cream:** Add ½ cup chopped semi-sweet chocolate chips.

• **Chocolate chip mint:** Add ½ cup chopped semi-sweet chocolate chips plus ¼ tsp. mint extract.

• **Rocky Road:** After ice cream has set, mix 1 cup mini marshmallows and ½ cup chopped pecans.

• **Moose Tracks:** Add ½ cup cocoa and ½ cup chocolate chunks to ice cream mixture before freezing.

No Ice Cream Maker Method:
To prepare recipe without an ice cream maker, place a 9x13 inch dish in freezer until cold. Prepare cream mixture as directed. Transfer to prepared dish. Freeze until edges of mixture begin to set, about 20-30 minutes. Using a hand mixer, beat until smooth. Freeze, covered, until firm, about 3 hours longer, beating again every 30 minutes.

2 Ingredient Fudge

2   cups (one 12 oz. bag) semi-sweet chocolate chips
1   (14 oz.) can sweetened condensed milk
2   Tbsp. butter (optional)

Pour ingredients into a microwave proof bowl. Melt in 30 second increments. Stir after each 30 seconds. When melted, pour into a greased 8x8 inch pan. Let cool in the fridge and then cut into pieces.

Variations

- **Nuts:** Add as desired.

- **Cherry Mash:** Use cherry chips to make to the fudge. Then pour melted semi-sweet chocolate chips on top. Sprinkle with chopped peanuts.

- **Peanut Butter:** Use peanut butter chips to make to the fudge. Then top with chocolate, if you like.

- **Dark Chocolate:** Use dark chocolate chips.

- **Mint:** Use mint chips, mint pieces or 1 tsp. mint flavoring.

- **Chocolate Covered Strawberry:** Stir in 2-3 Tbsp. of strawberry jam.

- **Rocky Road:** Stir in ½ cup marshmallows and ¼ cup chopped almonds.

- **Vanilla Fudge:** Use white chocolate chips instead.

- **Candy Cane:** Use white chocolate chips and stir in crushed candy canes.

- **M&M:** Stir in ⅓ cup of M&M's.

- **Spicy Mexican:** Add 1 tsp. cinnamon and ¼ tsp cayenne pepper.

- **Caramel:** Swirl ¼ cup caramel sauce on top.

- **S'more:** Layer, with graham crackers on bottom. Put fudge on top of graham crackers and top with marshmallows or marshmallow cream.

3 Ingredient Peanut Butter Fudge

3   cups white chocolate chips (or peanut butter chips)
1   (14 oz.) can sweetened condensed milk
     butter (optional)
2   Tbsp. peanut butter

Pour white chocolate chips and sweetened condensed milk into a microwave safe bowl. Melt in 30 second increments. Stir after each 30 seconds.

When melted, stir in butter for a creamier texture, if desired. Stir in peanut butter. Pour into a greased 8×8 inch pan. Let cool in the fridge and then cut into pieces.

Chocolate Peanut Clusters

1   cup semi-sweet chocolate chips
1   cup peanuts, walnuts, raisins or chopped dried apricots

Place chocolate chips in a microwave safe bowl and microwave on high 1-2 minutes, stirring halfway through cooking, until melted.

Stir in the nuts or dried fruit (or a combination of both).

Drop the mixture by the teaspoonful onto a waxed paper-lined baking sheet and refrigerate until firm. Store at a cool room temperature.

Makes 15 candies.

2 Ingredient Coconut Snowball Candy

1   cup white baking chips, melted
1   cup sweetened shredded coconut

Drop melted white chips by teaspoonfuls onto waxed paper or parchment paper. Roll in with coconut and let stand until dry.

Almond Joy Truffle

24 oz. shredded coconut
1   (14 oz.) can sweetened condensed milk
2   cups powdered sugar
1   tsp. vanilla
1½-2 cups whole almonds
4   cups (two 12 oz. bags) milk chocolate chips

Mix coconut, sweetened condensed milk, powdered sugar and vanilla until well blended. Drop by spoonfuls onto waxed paper or silicone baking mat.

Place 1 almond in the center of each ball and reform coconut mixture around the ball. You can use extra coconut to make it stiffer. Place in the freezer to set up for 15 minutes.

When coconut almond balls are set (they won't be hard), melt chocolate. Dip coconut almond balls in the melted chocolate. Place back on waxed paper and let harden in the fridge.

Peppermint Bark

1 lb. white almond bark
1 cup crushed peppermint candies*
¼-½ tsp. peppermint flavoring (optional)

Melt almond bark in the microwave according to the directions. Stir in peppermints and flavoring.

Pour onto waxed paper or a silicone baking mat on a cookie sheet. Spread and let harden. You can put it in the fridge if you prefer. Then break into pieces.

*To crush candy canes or other peppermint candies, put them in a ziptop bag and smash them with a rolling pin.

Variations

You can put just about anything into almond bark for different flavors! Here are some suggestions:

- Almonds
- Almonds and cherries
- Peanut butter chips
- Oreos
- M&M's
- Caramel bits

If robbers ever broke into my house and searched for money, I would just laugh and search with them.

Hard Candy

3½ cups sugar
1 cup light corn syrup
1 cup water
¼-½ tsp. cinnamon or peppermint oil*
1 tsp. red or green food coloring

In a large heavy saucepan, combine sugar, corn syrup and water. Cook on medium-high heat until candy thermometer reads 300° (hard-crack stage), stirring occasionally.

Remove from heat. Stir in flavoring oil and food coloring, keeping your face away from the mixture as the odor is very strong.

Immediately pour onto an oiled baking sheet. Cool. Break into pieces. Store in airtight containers.

* Cinnamon oil and peppermint oil are available in cake decorating and candy making supply stores.

I'm in a dark place right now.
Not emotionally-- I'm just in the
closet, hiding from the kids.

Notes

Notes

Miscellaneous

Miscellaneous Tips

- **When cooking, always read the recipe all the way through before you start.** This helps you make sure you have all the ingredients and you are cooking things in the right order.

- **Crackers are a mess to try to keep in the package and use when they're broken.** Keep a sealed jar to store cracker crumbs.

- **To keep apples crisp,** keep them in the refrigerator.

- **Save cereal box liners** to use to crush things like graham crackers, cornflakes or bread crumbs.

- **If you hate cooking at home but want to start saving money,** reward yourself by giving yourself a tip for each dinner you make. Place the same amount into a jar that you would leave as a tip if you went out to eat. At the end of the month, use that money for something special, like a kitchen appliance to make cooking easier, disposable pans, or something pretty for your kitchen.

- **Be sure to taste your food before you serve it.** This seems like a no brainer, but many people don't taste food before serving it to make sure it is seasoned properly.

- **Don't wear long sleeves while cooking** (like on a robe). They can catch fire or get into the hot mixture you are cooking.

- **Always turn your pan handles** so the pan doesn't accidentally get knocked off the stove.

- **When doing a lot of cooking or baking,** keep a trash can near you so it is easily accessible. You could also use a large bowl.

- **If you are going to be doing a lot of cooking,** pin a hand towel to your apron so you don't need to keep looking for your towel.

- **Don't spend money on an expensive microfiber dish drying mat** when a dish towel folded in half does the same thing.

Bread Crumbs

bread

Let bread dry out on the counter overnight. Place in a food processor and blend or smash until crumbs in a ziptop bag. Store in an airtight container.

Seasoned Butters
(For corn on the cob or other vegetables)

Here are a few tasty combinations for seasoned butter. Mix the amounts you want, according to your taste, into either softened or melted butter. You can also use these on roasted veggies or on the meats you are barbecuing.

- dried oregano, basil, garlic powder
- Italian seasoning mixed with grated Parmesan cheese
- lime juice and lime zest
- lemon juice and lemon zest
- chili powder with cumin or hot pepper sauce
- ranch dressing mix
- horseradish
- ¼ tsp. dry mustard and 1 tsp. fresh dill or ¼ tsp. dried dill

"Who needs floors clean enough to eat off of if you serve your food at the table?"

Clotted Cream

4   cups heavy cream (not ultra-pasteurized)*

Preheat oven to 175-180°. Pour cream into a shallow glass or ceramic baking dish (an 8 or 9 inch square pan is ideal). The cream should be about 1½ to 2 inches deep.

Place dish in preheated oven. Bake 12 hours. Do not stir. Carefully remove from oven and let cool to room temperature. Cover with plastic wrap and refrigerate overnight or until completely chilled.

Pull back a corner of the top layer of thickened cream. Carefully pour liquid underneath into a container to use for baking.

Store thickened (clotted) cream in a ceramic crock or canning jar. Cover and refrigerate up to 5 days. Serve with scones or toast.

*"They" say don't use ultra-pasteurized but I have and it's turned out fine.

Instructions For Making A Box Mix

1. Read directions on box.

2. Throw box away.

3. Pull box out of trash 15 seconds later.

4. Repeat

Greek Yogurt

1   gallon whole milk (must be whole)
3   Tbsp. unsweetened yogurt with live active cultures

In a large pot, heat the milk until it reaches at least 180°, stirring occasionally.

Once the mixture reaches 180°, remove it from the heat and allow it to cool to 110° to 115°. You can speed the cooling process by plunging it into an ice bath. Combine one cup of warmed milk with yogurt and stir gently to combine. Add this mixture back to the large batch of heated milk. Divide into quart jars if using an oven or heating pad.

For the next 5 to 10 hours, depending on desired flavor* and consistency, keep the yogurt between 110° and 115°.

Crockpot: Use a crockpot on low or warm, depending on your crockpot, with the thermometer tucked along the side.

Oven: Place in the oven with just the oven light on for 8 hours.

Heating Pad: Place on a heating pad on low setting for 8 hours (if you have a heating pad that will stay on that long).

*The key is to check it often. The longer you incubate the yogurt, the thicker and more tart it becomes. Do not stir the yogurt during incubation.

For Regular Yogurt

Cover the yogurt and refrigerate at least two hours before eating or straining, ideally overnight.

For Greek Yogurt

Place a fine mesh strainer on top of bowl and line strainer with a coffee filter. Let it sit in the refrigerator to drain the whey into the bowl for 3-8 hours, depending on how thick you want it. If it gets too thick, then just stir some whey back into it.

How to Dry Lemon Peel

First, wash your lemons. Then peel them with a vegetable peeler. Try to get just the rind, not including the white pith.

Dehydrator

Place the peels in a single layer in your dehydrator. Dry them for 10-12 hours at 95°.

Oven

Place the peels in a single layer on tray and put them in the oven at 200° for 25-30 minutes.

You'll know they are completely dry when they snap and don't bend.

How to Use Lemon Peels

- Use in tea.
- Use in homemade salad dressing.
- Mix with sugar and sprinkle over scones or other baked goods.
- Add to sugar cookies for a pop of flavor.
- Put a bit into the crumb topping for apple crisp.
- Add to vanilla or lemon pudding for some extra zip.
- Use to brighten the flavor of artichokes. Add to the cooking water.

For potpourri:
Leave whole and store in an airtight container until used.

For recipes:
Crush the peels and buzz them in your coffee grinder until you get a fine powder. Store the lemon peel powder in the fridge - it will keep for a year.

Cooking with dried lemon peel:
When substituting in a recipe, use 1 teaspoon dried peel for each tablespoon of fresh peel called for in your recipe.

Lemon pepper:
Combine 2 Tbsp. lemon peel powder and 1 Tbsp. pepper. Add 1 tsp. salt if desired.

Fry Sauce

1   cup + 2 Tbsp. mayonnaise
¼   cup sugar
½   tsp. salt
⅛   tsp. paprika
¼   tsp. ground mustard
½   tsp. onion powder
½   cup ketchup
2   Tbsp. vinegar
1½   tsp. Worcestershire sauce

Stir until well blended. Cover and refrigerate until chilled, about 30 minutes. Store in refrigerator.

Garlic Parmesan Sauce

½   cup butter, melted
½   cup grated Parmesan cheese
1   tsp. garlic powder
½   tsp. onion salt
¼   tsp. pepper

Mix butter, Parmesan cheese, garlic power, onion salt and pepper together in a bowl.

Who says I can't cook?
You obviously have not tasted my cereal.

Kansas City Barbecue Sauce

2	cups ketchup
2	cups tomato sauce
1¼	cups brown sugar, packed
1¼	cups red wine vinegar
½	cup molasses
4	tsp. hickory flavored liquid smoke
2	Tbsp. butter
½	tsp. garlic powder
½	tsp. onion powder
¼	tsp. chili powder
1	tsp. paprika
½	tsp. celery seed
¼	tsp. cinnamon
½	tsp. cayenne pepper
1	tsp. salt
1	tsp. pepper

Add ingredients to a saucepan. Stir until smooth. Simmer on low until thickened, about 20 minutes.

Brush sauce onto any kind of meat during the last 10 minutes of cooking.

Thicker sauce: Simmer longer.

Thinner sauce: Simmer for less time. The sauce can also be thinned using a bit of water, if necessary.

Honey Barbecue Sauce

1	cup ketchup
½	cup honey
¼	cup white vinegar
¼	cup molasses
1	tsp. liquid smoke flavoring
½	tsp. salt
½	tsp. pepper
¼	tsp. paprika
¼	tsp. chili powder
¼	tsp. onion powder
¼	tsp. garlic powder
¼	tsp. cayenne pepper

Add ingredients to a saucepan. Stir until smooth. Simmer on low until thickened, about 20 minutes.

White Barbecue Sauce

2	cups mayonnaise
½	cup apple cider vinegar
¼	cup prepared extra hot horseradish
2	Tbsp. lemon juice
1½	tsp. pepper
2	tsp. prepared yellow mustard
1	tsp. salt
½	tsp. cayenne pepper
¼	tsp. garlic powder

Mix everything together in a bowl. Whisk together thoroughly until creamy and smooth. Cover and refrigerate until ready to use.

Raspberry Chipotle Sauce

2	Tbsp. olive oil
2	large jalapeno peppers, seeded and diced
2	cloves garlic, minced or 2 tsp. minced garlic
4	tsp. adobo sauce*
2	cups fresh or frozen raspberries
½	cup apple cider vinegar
½	tsp. salt
¼	cup brown sugar
½	cup sugar

Heat olive oil in a skillet over medium heat. Stir in jalapenos. Cook until tender, about 5 minutes.

Mix in garlic and adobo sauce. Bring to a simmer. Stir the raspberries into the sauce. Cook until soft, about 3 minutes.

Stir in the vinegar, salt, brown sugar and sugar. Mix well. Simmer until thickened and reduced by half, about 15 minutes.

Allow to cool to room temperature before serving, about 20 minutes.

*Adobo sauce can be purchased in the Mexican food section of your grocery store.

Sometimes success is just getting the laundry into the dryer before it mildews.

Texas Roadhouse®
Honey Butter Copycat

1   cup butter, very soft
1   cup powdered sugar
1   cup honey
2   tsp. cinnamon

Add everything in the order listed, whipping well. Oh Yum!

Cinnamon Sour Cream

Use a dollop on top of spice cake or gingerbread in place of frosting.

¼   cup sour cream
2   tsp. sugar
⅛   tsp. cinnamon
    dash of nutmeg

Mix all ingredients and serve with fresh fruit.

You can use this as a fruit salad dressing, too. If used as a dressing, you can use canned fruit and garnish with coconut and/or toasted chopped almonds or nuts.

- **If honey becomes crystallized, don't throw it away. Warm it in the microwave or in a pan of boiling water. Stir it until it becomes clear.**

Mustard Spread

This is good as a sandwich spread. It also makes a great dip for cooked meats like chicken tenders, corn dogs, steak cubes or ham.

¼	cup butter or margarine, softened
2	Tbsp. ground mustard
2	Tbsp. vinegar
¼	tsp. garlic salt
4	drops hot pepper sauce (like Tabasco)

Mix and beat until smooth.

Spaghetti Seasoning Mix

¼	cup instant minced onion
¼	cup dried parsley
¼	cup cornstarch
1	Tbsp. dried green pepper flakes (optional)
1	Tbsp. salt
1	tsp. instant minced garlic
½	tsp. pepper
1	Tbsp. sugar
1	Tbsp. dried Italian seasoning

Mix ingredients. This equals 1 spaghetti seasoning mix packet from the store.

You can double, triple or quadruple this recipe to make it in bulk.

Greek Seasoning

1   Tbsp. basil, dried
1   Tbsp. dill, dried
2   Tbsp. garlic powder
1   Tbsp. onion flakes
2   Tbsp. oregano
1   Tbsp. parsley, dried
1   Tbsp. rosemary, dried
½   Tbsp. thyme
1   Tbsp. lemon pepper seasoning
½   Tbsp. marjoram
1   Tbsp. salt
½   Tbsp. pepper
½   Tbsp. cinnamon
½   Tbsp. nutmeg

Mix. Use on your favorite chicken or steak dish!

You can double, triple or quadruple this recipe to make it in bulk.

Fajita Seasoning

1   Tbsp. cornstarch
2   tsp. chili powder
1   tsp. salt
1   tsp. paprika
1   tsp. sugar
½   tsp. onion powder
½   tsp. garlic powder
¼   tsp. cayenne pepper
½   tsp. cumin

Mix. Store in a spice jar.

You can double, triple or quadruple this recipe to make it in bulk.

Southwest Seasoning

2   Tbsp. chili powder
2   tsp. cumin
2   Tbsp. paprika
1   tsp. pepper
1   Tbsp. ground coriander
1   tsp. cayenne pepper
1   Tbsp. garlic powder
1   tsp. crushed red pepper flakes
1   Tbsp. salt
1   Tbsp. dried oregano

Mix and store in a spice bottle.

You can double, triple or quadruple this recipe to make it in bulk.

Chili Mix

4   tsp. chili powder
1   Tbsp. crushed red pepper
1   Tbsp. dried minced onion
1   Tbsp. dried minced garlic
2   tsp. sugar
2   tsp. cumin
2   tsp. dried parsley
2   tsp. salt
1   tsp. basil
¼   tsp. pepper

Mix and store in a spice shaker.

You can double, triple or quadruple this recipe to make it in bulk.

- **To thicken chili, add 1-2 tablespoons cornstarch or flour to ½ cup cold water and stir. Add to chili and cook until thickened, about 5 minutes.**

Hamburger Seasoning

2	tsp.	paprika
1½	tsp.	pepper
1¼	tsp.	salt
½	tsp.	brown sugar
¼	tsp.	garlic powder
¼	tsp.	onion powder
¼	tsp.	cayenne pepper

Combine. Sprinkle on hamburger before cooking.

You can double, triple or quadruple this recipe to make it in bulk.

Lemon Pepper

5	large lemons
⅓	cup pepper
¼	cup sea salt or kosher salt (optional)

Zest all the lemons and mix zest with pepper.

Spread zest on parchment lined baking sheet and bake on lowest setting until the zest is completely dried. Add the lemon pepper to a spice grinder and grind until desired texture.

Mix with sea salt or kosher salt, if desired, and store in an airtight container for up to a few months.

You can double, triple or quadruple this recipe to make it in bulk.

Steak Dry Rub I

3   Tbsp. sea salt or kosher salt
3   Tbsp. smoked paprika
2   Tbsp. onion powder
2   Tbsp. garlic powder
2   Tbsp. oregano
2   Tbsp. pepper
1   Tbsp. brown sugar
1   Tbsp. cumin

Mix and store in a spice bottle. Can be doubled or tripled to make in bulk. Cover meat with the spice blend and rub deeply into the meat. Allow meat to sit for 15-20 minutes before grilling.

You can double, triple or quadruple this recipe to make it in bulk.

Steak Dry Rub II

1   Tbsp. sea salt or kosher salt
1   Tbsp. brown sugar, packed
2   tsp. smoked paprika
2   tsp. ground ancho chile pepper*
1   tsp. thyme
1   tsp. pepper
½   tsp. garlic powder
½   tsp. onion powder
½   tsp. ground mustard
½   tsp. cumin

Mix. Makes enough to season 4 large steaks.

When ready to use, rub the seasoning over all sides of the steaks, and allow them to rest at least 20 minutes before grilling or searing.

*Can be purchased in the Mexican food section of your grocery store.

You can double, triple or quadruple this recipe to make it in bulk.

Tennessee Dry Rub

¾ cup dark brown sugar, packed
¾ cup sugar
½ cup sweet paprika
¼ cup garlic powder
2 Tbsp. pepper
2 Tbsp. ground ginger powder
2 Tbsp. onion powder
2 tsp. rosemary powder*

Mix.

To Use: Sprinkle meat with salt and 2 tablespoons rub up to 12 hours in advance.

*Grind rosemary into a powder with a mini blender or mortar and pestle.

You can double, triple or quadruple this recipe to make it in bulk.

Montreal Steak Seasoning

2 Tbsp. paprika
2 Tbsp. pepper
2 Tbsp. sea salt or kosher salt
1 Tbsp. garlic powder
1 Tbsp. onion powder
1 Tbsp. crushed coriander
1 Tbsp. dill
1 Tbsp. crushed red pepper flakes

Mix and store in a spice jar.

You can double, triple or quadruple this recipe to make it in bulk.

Cajun Seasoning

2   tsp. salt
2   tsp. garlic powder
2½   tsp. paprika
1   tsp. pepper
1   tsp. onion powder
1   tsp. cayenne pepper
1¼   tsp. dried oregano
1¼   tsp. thyme
½   tsp. red pepper flakes (optional)

Mix and store in a spice bottle.

You can double, triple or quadruple this recipe to make it in bulk.

Adobo Seasoning

2   Tbsp. salt
1   Tbsp. paprika
2   tsp. pepper
1½   tsp. onion powder
1½   tsp. dried oregano
1½   tsp. cumin
1   tsp. garlic powder
1   tsp. chili powder

Mix. Store in a spice jar.

You can double, triple or quadruple this recipe to make it in bulk.

I just burned 1200 calories.
I forgot the pizza in the oven.

Mrs. Dash® Copycat

½   tsp. cayenne pepper
1   Tbsp. garlic powder
1   tsp. basil
1   tsp. marjoram
1   tsp. thyme
1   tsp. parsley
1   tsp. savory
1   tsp. mace
1   tsp. onion powder
1   tsp. sage
1   tsp. pepper

Mix. Store in a spice bottle.

You can double, triple or quadruple this recipe to make it in bulk.

Salt Free Seasoning Mix

2   tsp. celery seed
2   tsp. Italian seasoning
2   tsp. dried parsley
1   tsp. poppy seeds
1   tsp. pepper
1   tsp. onion powder
1   tsp. red pepper flakes
¾   tsp. garlic powder
¾   tsp. paprika

Mix and store in a spice jar.

You can double, triple or quadruple this recipe to make it in bulk.

Jerk Seasoning Mix

1	Tbsp. allspice
¼	tsp. cinnamon
¼	cup brown sugar
1	tsp. red pepper flakes
¼	tsp. ground cloves
¼	tsp. cumin
2	tsp. salt
1	tsp. pepper
2	Tbsp. canola oil

Mix spices with oil. Rub on meat and refrigerate from 2 hours to overnight before cooking.

You can double, triple or quadruple this recipe to make it in bulk.

Sazon Seasoning Mix

1	Tbsp. ground coriander
1	Tbsp. ground cumin
1	Tbsp. ground annatto seeds (achiote) or turmeric
1	Tbsp. garlic powder
1	Tbsp. sea salt or kosher salt
2	tsp. ground oregano
1	tsp. pepper

Combine all ingredients and mix well. Store in an airtight container.
1½ tsp. of this mix equals one packet of commercial sazon.

You can double, triple or quadruple this recipe to make it in bulk.

Everything Bagels Seasoning

2   Tbsp. poppy seeds
2   Tbsp. white sesame seeds or
       1 Tbsp. white and Tbsp. black sesame seeds
1½ Tbsp. dried minced onion
1   Tbsp. dried minced garlic
½   Tbsp. flaked or coarse sea salt or kosher salt

Mix.

You can double, triple or quadruple this recipe to make it in bulk.

Hospitality is making your guests feel at home, even though you wish they were.

Chex Mix

3   cups Corn Chex cereal
3   cups Rice Chex cereal
1½   cups Wheat Chex cereal
1½   cups oyster crackers*
1   cup cheese crackers*
1   cup pretzel twists*
1   cup mixed nuts (optional)
6   Tbsp. butter or margarine, melted
2   Tbsp. Worcestershire sauce
1½   tsp. seasoned salt
¾   tsp. onion powder

Place the cereal, crackers, pretzels and nuts into a large microwave safe bowl.

Mix together the melted butter, Worcestershire sauce, seasoned salt and onion powder.

Pour the butter mixture over the cereal and toss to coat evenly.

Oven: Bake at 350° for 1 hour, stirring every 15 minutes.

Microwave: Microwave for 5-6 minutes, stirring thoroughly every 2 minutes. Then spread onto paper towels to cool.

Serve immediately or store in a sealed container for up to 1 week.

*Mix and match any crackers or cereal you want:

Cheerios
Honey Nut Cheerios
rye crisps
bagel chips
mini breadsticks
crunchy Cheetos

Notes

Cleaning

How To Season A Cast Iron Pan

Oven Method

Step 1
Scour inside and outside of pan with steel wool pad with soap. This will be the only time you use soap or a steel wool pad on the pan.

Step 2
Rinse and dry.

Step 3
Coat inside and out with a thin layer of solid shortening or vegetable oil (shortening is best).

Step 4
Place in an oven on a foil covered rack at 350°. Make sure pans are turned upside down on foil. Bake 1-2 hours. Turn off oven and let cool in oven.

Step 5
Coat once more with shortening or vegetable oil. Store in a dry place.

Stovetop Method

Step 1
Clean pan with ½ inch of oil and a thick layer of salt.

Step 2
With salt mix still in pan, heat on high until oil starts to smoke.

Step 3
Carefully discard oil.

Step 4
With rag or paper towels, wipe the inside of the pan clean.

How To Clean
A Cast Iron Pan

Step 1
While pan is still hot, rinse and wash pan with hot water* (no soap). Use a scrub brush and coarse salt for stuck-on food.

For extra stubborn food residue, boil water in the pan to loosen.

Step 2
Dry immediately with a towel or dry on the stove over low heat to prevent rust.

Step 3
Rub inside of pan with thin coat of shortening (shortening is best).

Step 4
Store in a dry place.

*NEVER allow cast iron pan to soak in water for any amount of time. It will rust.

If you wait long enough to make dinner, everyone will eat cereal.

How To Clean A Burned Pan

For stainless steel and aluminum pans:

Method 1: Scrub with an SOS pad. If that doesn't work:

Method 2: Place a generous amount of baking soda (about ½ cup) in the bottom of the pan. Make sure it covers the bottom. Fill with water and simmer for an hour or so. Most of the burned stuff should come right off. You can do this more than once if needed.

Method 3: If it doesn't all come off with the other methods, scrape off the last of the burned-on food with a razor blade.

Method 4 (Stainless steel only): Spray with oven cleaner and let sit 1 hour before cleaning with an SOS or scratchy pad.

Method 5: (Reader Tip from Charley) Here's how to clean the outside of a pot or pan. Spray WD-40 on the outside of the pan. Let it soak for 10 minutes. Then remove the burned-on grease. Be sure to wash it thoroughly with soap and water before using! This works really well. It also works very well on the backyard grill grates that are always really dirty with burned-on grease and food! They really come clean!!!

For non-stick pans:

Place a generous amount of baking soda (about ½ cup) in the bottom of the pan. Make sure it covers the bottom. Fill with water and simmer for an hour or so. Most of the burned stuff should rinse right off. You can do this more than once if needed.

Note from Jill

My son-in-law (Mike) just called and said, "How do you react when you ask your wife (Tawra), "What is this burned-on stuff that I can't get off this pan?" and she casually answers, "Oh, that is just carpet burned-on in that spot". (At this point, my son-in-law and I are having a good belly laugh.) How many people do you know who have gotten burned carpet stuck on a pan lately?
...only Tawra.

Other Burned Pan Options

Burned Pan Recipe #1

In the pan, place about:

1	inch water
1	Tbsp. baking soda
2-3	Tbsp. hydrogen peroxide
1-2	drops liquid dish detergent
	(no more or it will bubble like crazy)

Boil (don't simmer) 10-15 minutes. Check it to make sure it doesn't boil dry. If necessary, just add a little more water.

Burned Pan Recipe #2

In a pan, place:

1	inch of water
	dishwasher detergent tablet or
	1-2 Tbsp. powdered dishwasher soap
1	Tbsp. baking soda
2-3	Tbsp. vinegar

Boil (don't simmer) 10-15 minutes.

> My cooking is so awesome, even the smoke alarm cheers me on.

How To Clean A Ceramic/Glass Stovetop

Supplies needed:

baking soda
dish soap
razor blade scraper
Scotch Brite or Chore Boy scratchy pad

After stovetop has cooled, wipe as much as you can with a wet wash cloth and some dish soap.

Holding your scraper at an angle, scrape off as much burned-on food as possible. About 90% of the burned-on food will come off simply by scraping.

Afterward, you will have what looks like a big mess. Wipe it clean with an OLD rag and then you can see what's left to scour.

Scour with grease-cutting dish soap (like Dawn) and a Chore Boy or green scratchy pad. Scotch Brite green scratchy pads work the best. Just squirt a little dish soap on it and then scrub away.

If you don't have a green scratchy pad or a Chore Boy, you can use baking soda. Pour a little baking soda on a wet rag. Then scrub until all the burned food is off. You may need to scrub several times to get it all off.

When finished, wipe with a clean wet rag until all baking soda residue is gone.

Note from Tawra: If you follow the maintenance cleaning, you should only have to do this when you have a really bad, burned-on spill, which usually only happens once or twice a year for me.

Keeping Your Stovetop Sparkling Clean

Clean it right away - As soon as your stove is cool, wipe it right away with soap and a dish rag.

Clean it every day - If you wipe the stovetop each day after you're done cooking, it will be a lot quicker. It will take 30 seconds, rather than spending 5 minutes doing a big clean up.

Let it soak - If something is stuck-on, you can pour a little water on the stovetop and let it soak while you are doing your dishes. A lot of times, this will make it easy to wipe everything off. If the water spreads too much, you can lay a wet rag on the spot to soak it.

How To Clean An Oven

Method 1: Self-cleaning ovens. Nuff said. -Mike (just kidding!)

Remove large chunks out of oven.*

Turn on self-cleaning oven. If your oven has a "high" and "low" setting start with "low" first.

When cooled, wipe down ash from inside oven.

*If you are using the self cleaning method and you leave the large chunks in the oven, you will have a fire in the oven and smoke up your entire house. (Ask Mike how Tawra knows. ;-)

Method 2: Buy a can of oven cleaner.

Oven cleaner is very potent, so wear a small face mask or stand back when spraying to avoid inhaling the fumes.

Using gloves, spray liberally all over the inside of the oven. Let it sit 1-3 hours; Then wipe with a wet cloth.

Method 3: Buy a new oven. -Mike (Ask me how I know. ;-)

How To Clean A
Stainless Steel Sink

Step 1: Get the gross OFF! Use a solution of dish soap and water to wipe down all the food and grime. Do not rinse. Let it soak for 1-5 minutes, until it loosens all the stuck-on food. When everything is softened, wipe out the sink with fresh water.

You can skip this step if your sink isn't too bad, but it's a good idea to do it if you have a lot of stuck-on food.

Step 2: Scrub it! Use either a stainless steel cleaner or baking soda and vinegar. Bar Keepers Friend is a good inexpensive stainless steel cleaner brand, which does not contain bleach.

(If you use a cleaner with bleach, like Comet, you must immediately rinse your sink or the bleach can pit your stainless steel sink.)

Stainless steel cleaner: Just rub on and rinse.

Baking soda and vinegar: Scrub the sink with baking soda first. When you're finished scrubbing, leave the baking soda on. Then pour some vinegar over the sink and let it bubble. Rinse with water.

IMPORTANT: When you're cleaning the sink, make sure you wipe around the edges and the back of the faucet. A lot of people miss this area. This is where a lot of gross stuff can collect, causing unpleasant odors, and the grime can build up over time so that you will have to scrape it off.

If you have missed this area a lot and you have a big buildup, you can take a plastic scraper like a pot scraper or a plastic knife and scrape away the buildup.

Step 3: Dry the sink. Wipe down the clean sink and counters with a dry cloth. This makes the sink look shiny and extra clean.

Step 4: Shine It! To add even more shine to your stainless steel sink, wipe down with a small amount of olive oil or mineral oil and shine with a dry cloth.

#1 Tip For Keeping Your Sink Always Looking Good

WIPE IT DOWN IMMEDIATELY AFTER EVERY LOAD OF DISHES!!! Seriously! It takes about 30 seconds to wipe and dry your sink and if you do this every time, it will keep the grime from building up. While you're at it, make sure to wipe the counters, too, and be sure to dry them. Towel drying makes counters look shiny and extra clean, just like it does with the sinks.

To Freshen Your Garbage Disposal

To freshen your garbage disposal, you can put a piece of lemon or orange peel in the disposal and run it. The lemon will help clean and freshen, so if you have odors you might try this.

Smelly Sink?

To prevent smells, run your garbage disposal at least every week.

Sinks do not just start smelling on their own. There is something like food or a rag stuck in there allowing the bacteria to grow in the warm, moist environment. You must remove the cause before the smell will go away. Often, chemicals like Drano will not permanently solve the problem. You must remove the object that is holding the bacteria.

If your sink is smelling like a dead animal and draining slowly: **With the disposal off!!,** put your hand (gloves optional) in the sink and feel around to see if you have a washrag, sponge or extra large piece of food stuck in your disposal. If so, remove it. :-) Nine times out of ten, this is what is causing smelly, slow draining sinks.

If you don't find anything, you will need to remove the trap under the sink. (The u-shaped part at the bottom of the pipes is the trap - Google it.) You more than likely have something stuck in the trap. For bathroom sinks, this is often hair and body grease. Remove anything that is not part of the pipe and replace the trap.

How To Clean
Stainless Steel Appliances

Wipe with hot soapy water and dry with a towel.

To remove stuck-on food, saturate a rag with hot, soapy water and let it sit on the spot until the food is softened.

To disinfect and shine, add rubbing alcohol to the hot soapy water or spray rubbing alcohol on appliances and wipe dry.

How To Clean
Granite Countertops

Wipe with hot soapy water and dry with a towel.

To remove stuck-on food, saturate a rag with hot, soapy water and let it sit on the spot until the food is softened.

To disinfect, add rubbing alcohol to the hot soapy water or spray rubbing alcohol on counters and wipe dry.

How To Clean
Marble Countertops

Wipe with hot water and dry with a towel. Soap can dull marble, so use it sparingly.

To remove stuck-on food, saturate a rag with hot water and let it sit on the spot until food is softened.

Carpet Cleaner 1

2   Tbsp. Tide liquid laundry detergent
¼   cup Awesome cleaner (dollar store)
1   scoop Oxiclean
1   gallon hot water

In a 1-gallon container, combine Tide, Awesome cleaner and Oxiclean. Stir together with a spoon until well combined. Slowly pour the hot water into the cleaning solution, so you don't make too many bubbles. Stir until dissolved.

Thoroughly vacuum the carpet.

Read the directions that came with your carpet cleaning machine for how much cleaner to add. Some reservoirs are smaller than others. For typical carpet shampoo machines, pour ¼ cup of this concentrated solution into your carpet shampoo machine reservoir. Then fill the rest of the reservoir with hot water. (**The ratio I use is about a gallon of hot water to ¼ cup of this concentrated cleaning solution.)

Before using carpet cleaner, test on a less visible area of flooring to make sure it's safe for your carpet and wait at least 24 hours for the test spot to dry to see the results.

Instead of cleaning, I just watched an episode of hoarders. I didn't realize how fantastic my house looks.

Carpet Cleaner 2

1   Tbsp. clear dishwashing liquid (non-moisturizing)
¼   cup ammonia
¼   cup vinegar
1   gallon water

Combine ingredients in a 1 gallon container. Stir together with a spoon until well combined.

Thoroughly vacuum carpet.

Read the directions that came with your carpet cleaning machine for how much cleaner to add. Some reservoirs are smaller than others. For typical carpet shampoo machines, pour ¼ cup of this concentrated solution into your carpet shampoo machine reservoir. Then fill the rest of the reservoir with hot water. (**The ratio I use is about a gallon of hot water to ¼ cup of this concentrated cleaning solution.)

Before using carpet cleaner, test on a less visible area of flooring to make sure it's safe for your carpet and wait at least 24 hours for the test spot to dry to see the results.

Spot Carpet Cleaner

6   oz. hydrogen peroxide (3% solution)
2   oz. Dawn dish soap (blue - original formula)

Mix. Spray in a hidden area to test on carpet first. Rinse with a rag with water. Wait 24 hours to make sure it doesn't bleach your carpet. If it's ok, then use it to treat spots on your carpet.

Dog Urine Cleaner

vinegar

Douse urine spot with straight vinegar so it is VERY saturated. Place a folded up towel over the spot. Place something heavy on top of the towel like the vinegar bottle and leave overnight to soak up the vinegar. Remove towel. The smell will be gone in the morning.

Soft Scrubbing Cleaner

¾   cup baking soda
¼   cup dish soap (Dawn works best)
1   Tbsp. water
10-15 drops lemon or tea tree essential oil (optional)

Combine ingredients and mix. Stir until you achieve a paste-like consistency. Add a little more baking soda, if needed, to get the consistency you want.

Wood Floor Cleaner

¾   cup vinegar
¾   cup isopropyl alcohol
2-3   drops dish soap

Mix in a spray bottle and fill to top with water.

Febreze® Copycat

½   cup vinegar
¼   cup rubbing alcohol
5-10 drops essential oil

Mix everything in a spray bottle and fill to the top with water.

Foaming Soap Refill

2   Tbsp. regular liquid hand soap or bubble bath
     enough water to top off the bottle

Pour the liquid hand soap in the bottle and fill to the top with water. Swirl it around gently until it's mixed and you have foaming hand soap!

Air Freshener

1   Tbsp. isopropyl alcohol
30   drops essential oil or fragrance oil
½   cup distilled water

Mix in spray bottle.

If I don't clean my house soon, someone is going to bring in blindfolded people for a Febreze commercial.

Toilet Bombs

1 cup baking soda
¼ cup citric acid
1 Tbsp. rubbing alcohol
20 drops essential oil or fragrance oil of your choice
    (citrus or lavender are popular)

Mix baking soda and citric acid together in a small bowl. Drop rubbing alcohol and essential oils over the baking soda and citric acid. Stir the mixture and continue to drop alcohol and essential oils until moistened.

Scoop your toilet bombs out using a teaspoon or pack tightly into silicone ice cube trays. Carefully place each bomb on a cookie sheet. It'll harden up when it's dry. Spray the top of the toilet bombs with more rubbing alcohol. This step is important because it helps to harden the bombs so they don't crumble. Let dry for 4-6 hours.

Once your toilet bombs are dry, you can store them in a container.

Variation

• **Toilet Tea:** Mix ingredients for toilet bombs. Store in a jar. To use, put 1-2 tablespoons in toilet water.

How To Clean Your Front Load Washing Machine

I've NEVER, EVER had to clean my HE washer. I didn't even know it could get moldy!

I admit, it disturbed me. I just kept wondering, "Why do other people's washers get that gross but mine doesn't?" Well I have finally come up with the answer. Do you want to know my secret??

Drumroll please...

I use bleach and the sanitary cycle to clean my whites once a week. Seriously- that's it! I don't do anything but that and it works! It works great! I've never ever bought any special cleaners and I've never ever had to clean my front loading HE washer because I bleach my whites.

I know that not everyone likes bleach, so I've added some tips on how to clean the inside of your washer if you don't want to use bleach on your clothes. You will NEVER have to spend money on washing machine cleaning tablets ever again. Really those are just a gimmick to get you to buy more stuff anyway.

I don't mean to brag, but today I washed AND dried a load of clothes without forgetting I had stuff in the washer. It is like I am now some kind of domestic ninja.

Solution #1 -
Run a load of whites with bleach or run an empty load with 1 cup bleach on the hottest setting you can use. Wipe the washing machine down with a bleach water solution. Pull back the rubber seal and wipe inside there too. Rinse.

Solution #2 -
Homemade Natural HE Washer Cleaner

2 cups vinegar*
1 cup baking soda

Pour vinegar in the detergent compartment. Pour baking soda into drum of washer and use hottest water setting possible.

*You really need to use bleach to clean your washer. There is mold building up inside and vinegar has been proven to NOT kill mold like bleach does. The vinegar does help to break down soap scum and reduce smell, but it will not kill the mold building up inside.
.

Solution #3 -
Add ½ cup dishwasher detergent to your washer, either with white clothes or without clothes and run on the hottest setting.

Additional High Efficiency Washer Tip

Be sure you aren't using too much laundry detergent and that you use the right kind of laundry detergent. With laundry detergent, more is NOT better. Soap buildup will cause the bacteria to build up too.

> I don't want to fold the laundry so I will restart the dryer 3 times in a row.

Disinfecting
Orange Cleaner

2 cups white vinegar
4 orange peels, clean off all fruit
½ cup rubbing alcohol*
  distilled water (optional)

Make sure that the peels have no traces of fruit left. Add to mason jar. Add in white vinegar.

Close the lid tightly and let it sit in a dark and cool place for 2 weeks.

Remove orange peels. Add rubbing alcohol. Use, as needed, as-is or dilute with distilled water to clean your home surfaces.

*Vinegar does not disinfect, so adding rubbing alcohol will help make this a disinfectant.

A surefire way to get rich quick-count your blessings.

Underarm Stain Remover

½   cup Dawn dish soap (only Dawn)
1   cup hydrogen peroxide
    baking soda

Mix Dawn and peroxide. Store in a container.

To use on white clothes: Spread some Dawn peroxide mixture onto the stain. Sprinkle baking soda on top. Take a brush and scrub it into the fabric. Let sit one hour and then laundry as usual.

Wrinkle Release Spray

2   cups water
1½ Tbsp. fabric softener

Mix and spray clothes lightly.

Ironing Spray Starch

1   heaping Tbsp. cornstarch
1   pint distilled warm water
1-2 drops essential or fragrance oil (optional)

Mix cornstarch and fragrance oil in water. Pour into a spray bottle. Shake before using.

Notes

Health & Beauty

Homemade Cough Syrup

4	Tbsp. hot water
2	Tbsp. apple cider vinegar
2	Tbsp. honey
½	tsp. cayenne pepper
½	tsp. ground ginger
½	tsp. cinnamon

Place all ingredients in a small glass jar. Secure the lid and shake well to combine.

Take 2 tsp. as often as needed.

Elderberry Syrup

½	cup dried elderberries or 1½ cups fresh elderberries
2	cups water
1	Tbsp. fresh ginger, minced (optional)
½	cup honey

Combine the elderberries, water, and ginger in a small saucepan over high heat. Bring the mixture to a boil. Lower the heat and allow the mixture to simmer until the water has been reduced by half, about 45 minutes.

Transfer the cooked berries and liquid to a clean bowl and pour it through a fine mesh strainer to remove the berry skins. Use the back of a spoon to press on the berries in the strainer to extract all of the juice. Then discard the small amount of pulp left in the strainer.

Allow the elderberry juice to cool to room temperature. Stir in honey. Use a whisk to incorporate it smoothly. Then transfer the syrup into a sealed glass jar that you can store in the fridge.

Store in the refrigerator for 2-3 months or freeze in ice cube trays to use after that.

Homemade Bug Repellent Bars

1   cup olive oil
1   cup avocado oil
1   cup beeswax
30-40 drops essential oils (any combination you like):
        citronella
        eucalyptus
        lavender
        peppermint
        lemon
        lemongrass
        clove oil

I like a combination of clove, citronella and lemon for my bug repellent bars.

Melt all of the ingredients together and stir until beeswax is melted. Add essential oils. Then pour into molds. Silicone molds work great. Let set until the bars are completely firm. Pop the bars out of the molds. Then just rub on your skin like a lotion.

> I wish I lived in a world where mosquitoes would suck fat instead of blood.

Large Ice Pack

2   cups water
1   cup rubbing alcohol

Mix in a zip top bag*. I suggest double bagging it. Freeze. You can use it over and over. The heavy duty freezer bags seem to work best for this homemade ice pack.

*When filling a bag with liquid or anything, place the bag in a bowl and fold the bag edges down over the bowl top. Then pour the liquid in.

Dish Soap Ice Pack

Fill a zip top bag ½-¾ full with dish soap. Double bag. Then freeze. You will be able to mold it around your injury. Heavy duty freezer bags last the longest.

Mosquito & Tick Repellent

4   oz. distilled water
2   oz. witch hazel or rubbing alcohol*
2   oz. castor oil*
5   drops cinnamon oil
15   drops eucalyptus oil
15   drops citronella oil

Combine all of the ingredients in a spray bottle. Be sure to shake well before each application.

*You can purchase these items in the pharmacy at your store.

Homemade Toothpaste

1   tsp. coconut oil, melted
7   Tbsp. white clay (kaolin or bentonite clay)
3   Tbsp. distilled water
15   drops of peppermint essential oil, optional
3   tsp. Xylitol (optional)
1   tsp. baking soda

Melt coconut oil. Once melted, add all the ingredients except the water. Once everything is well-combined, slowly add the water until it forms a thick paste.

Homemade Whitening Toothpaste

¼   cup baking soda
⅓   cup hydrogen peroxide
12   drops peppermint essential oils

Mix together until it forms a thick paste. Brush 1 time each week with this mixture.

> People who can finish the shampoo bottle and conditioner at the same time are truly gifted.

Whitening Charcoal Toothpaste

2   Tbsp. coconut oil
½   tsp. activated charcoal powder
2   Tbsp. baking soda
1-2 drops peppermint essential oil (optional)

Melt the coconut oil and mix in the activated charcoal, baking soda and essential oil. Pour the mixture into a small container and store in a cool dry place.

How To Use

Use whitening toothpaste 1 time a week.

Homemade Deodorant

½   cup baking soda
½   cup arrowroot powder or cornstarch
5   Tbsp. coconut oil
20   drops of grapefruit essential oil, or another essential oil with antibacterial properties

Mix baking soda and arrowroot together. Add coconut and essential oils and mix well. Pour into a clean, airtight jar.

Homemade deodorant will last 3-6 months in an airtight container.

A pea-sized amount under each arm is usually good.

Vick's® Shower Disks Copycat

1   cup baking soda
½   cup cornstarch*
⅓-½ cup water (You may need to add more or less.)
15   drops of eucalyptus essential oil or
       2-3 tsp. Vick's Vapor Rub** (you can also add other
       oils like peppermint or camphor, 15 drops each)

Mix, using enough water to make a thick paste. You can pour into muffin tins lined with papers, make small balls and set on a plate or put into a silicone ice cube tray or muffin tray. Let them set for at least 12 hours or overnight to AIR dry on counter. Remove from papers or silicone trays and store in an airtight container.

When ready to use, place a disk on the floor of your shower and let the water run on it while showering.

*You can leave the cornstarch out of them. I put it in because it helps hold them together better.

**Essential oils can be expensive. If you don't want to buy a lot of oils for this recipe, you can buy 1 bottle of the generic vapor rub and just use a couple of teaspoons in this mixture instead.

Deep thought for the day

When you clean a vacuum cleaner,
you become a vacuum cleaner.

Acne Face Wash

      baby shampoo
1   Tbsp. activated charcoal powder
10   drops tea tree oil

Fill a pump bottle ¾ full with baby shampoo. Add activated charcoal and tea tree oil to bottle. Shake to mix. Use twice a day.

Charcoal Face Mask

½   cup bentonite clay
1   cup activated charcoal powder

Mix ingredients.

To use: Mix 2 tsp. mask powder with 2 tsp. water. Spread on face and let sit until dry. Remove with water.

Thank you for your concern but no, I am not sick, dying or sad. I just put eye make-up on this morning.

Headache Relief

3   Tbsp. beeswax
2   Tbsp. coconut oil
2   Tbsp. almond oil (jojoba oil works well too)
8   drops frankincense essential oil
10   drops peppermint essential oil
6   drops spearmint essential oil
6   drops lavender essential oil
8   drops basil essential oil

Place beeswax, coconut oil and almond oil in a microwave-safe measuring cup. Microwave at 30 second intervals until melted. Add essential oils and mix. Pour into jars. Apply a pea-sized amount on temples or the back of the neck.

Lemon Sugar Scrub

½   cup sugar
     olive oil (enough to make a paste)
½   tsp. lemon essential oil
1   tsp. dried peppermint leaves (optional)
1-2 Tbsp. lemon peel powder (optional) (p. 329)

Mix and store in a wide-mouth jar.

Wet your body in the shower, massage a scoop of the sugar mix all over your skin, and rinse. Careful! The shower will be slippery!

Body Butter

½   cup shea butter
¼   cup cocoa butter
2   Tbsp. avocado oil
2   Tbsp. coconut oil
15   drops essential or fragrance oil

Melt shea butter and cocoa butter. Stir in avocado oil and coconut oil. Stir until the coconut oil has melted. Stir in fragrance. Store in jars.

Sleep Balm

1   Tbsp. beeswax pellets
1   Tbsp. jojoba oil
2   Tbsp. coconut oil
30   drops lavender essential oil
30   drops ylang-ylang essential oil
20   drops sweet marjoram oil

Melt oils and beeswax. Add essential oils. Store in small metal or glass tins or in lip balm tubes. Rub on the bottoms of your feet or on your chest before bed.

Eyeglass Cleaner

Fill a small spray bottle with:

½   isopropyl alcohol
½   water
1   drop of dish soap (optional)

Gently shake. Spray on eyeglasses and wipe with a clean 100% cotton cloth.

How To Heal Dry Feet And Cracked Heels

2% Salicylic Acid (acne pads or acne cream*)
Gold Bond Ultimate Healing With Skin Therapy cream

Wipe feet with acne pad or spread a thin layer of acne cream on feet. Then spread Gold Bond cream on feet. Put on socks. Repeat each night until feet are healed.

That's it! The Salicylic Acid is an exfoliant and it helps get rid of the dead skin on your dry feet and cracked heels. Then the Gold Bond Ultimate Healing Cream moisturizes so that the dry skin and cracked heels don't come back. When I tried this the FIRST night I noticed a big difference. My feet aren't horrid by any means but they were dry and and starting to crack and not look so great so I was very happy for this easy treatment.

*2% Salicylic Acid is just acne medicine. You can get it in the pads, cleanser or as a toner. I have used all of them and they all worked great.

By the way, Gold Bond Ultimate Healing Cream is the stuff that Mike LOVES to use in the winter. His hands get really badly cracked and bleed without it. I've never tried it because I always have a ton of other lotion to use up, but I'm planning to use this one from now on! (Can I get them to pay me to be a spokesperson?! LOL)

-Tawra

I had almost given up on anything working on any area of my body after trying so many things, but last night as I crawled into bed I rubbed an acne pad Tawra had given me over my feet. I didn't expect anything to happen at all but during the night I rubbed my feet together and they were as soft as a little baby's bottom. I was shocked!

-Jill

Help With Dry Feet In Diabetics

After I figured out my tip on the previous page, I was going though e-mail tips and found this tip from one of our faithful readers, Rose. I wanted to share her tip for helping diabetic feet.

Rose writes: My hubby, who is disabled and has diabetes, was told by his foot doctor to make sure to put a lotion on his foot. (He is an amputee and has only one leg.) The doctor told him to make sure the lotion has cocoa butter, aloe vera and vitamin E in it.

I went to 2 different places (Walmart and Walgreens) and both pharmacists said they didn't have any kind of lotion with all three of those ingredients, but both recommended this one brand (highly recommended) for diabetics who have severely dry feet. It is Gold Bond Ultimate Healing with Skin Therapy Cream. It has 7 intense moisturizers. I got the one with aloe. It also has vitamins A, C and E. It does penetrate fast, it is non greasy (big plus because I hate greasy lotions!) and it has a nice scent.

Normally, I don't like to recommend stuff like this (especially lotions, because everyone seems to have his or her own favorite) but last night I used a bit of this on my own feet and I must share with you all that my feet feel so soft and smooth! (I have diabetes, too, so I do suffer from very dry feet.) Normally, when I do put lotion on my feet, they feel dry the next day (really no improvement) but almost 24 hours after putting on the Gold Bond Ultimate Healing, my feet feel like I just put lotion on them.

I bought the Gold Bond at Walmart. (It's cheaper there.) I paid less than $6, but this is for 2 people and hubby and I won't use this every day… In fact, I bought it 4 days ago and used it once on him and now once on me so we expect to use it just once every 5 days.

-Rose

Shoe Deodorizing Powder I

zinc oxide

Put zinc powder in an old spice bottle with a shaker. Shake into shoes as needed.

This is my #1 favorite foot powder. You can get zinc oxide cheaply on Amazon.

Shoe Deodorizing Powder II

6   Tbsp. cornstarch or arrowroot powder
3   Tbsp. baking soda
5-10   drops tea tree oil (optional)
5 -10 drops eucalyptus oil (optional)
10-15 drops peppermint oil (optional)

Mix and put in an old spice bottle with a shaker. Sprinkle in shoes and on feet as needed.

Notes

Notes

Kids

Puffy Paint

3   cups shaving cream (foam not gel - more, if needed)
1   cup all purpose flour
1   cup white glue, such as Elmer's glue
      food coloring or paint

Put shaving cream, flour and glue into a large mixing bowl. Mix together without overmixing. (You want to keep the air bubbles in the shaving cream.

Divide the white puffy paint mixture between 3 to 4 small bowls. Add a few drops of food coloring or paint to each bowl, stirring in, but again being careful not to overmix.

Spoon the puffy paint into sandwich bags. Seal each bag. (Add duct tape as well to help keep it closed if your kids are extra vigorous squeezers.) Then cut a small corner off. Squeeze the foam paint through the small hole onto your paper or board, making puffy lines, dots, and designs as desired.

Edible Puffy Paint

1   jar marshmallow cream (or marshmallow fluff)
      food coloring

Mix a couple drops of food coloring into marshmallow cream to the desired color.

This is messy so it doesn't make a good finger paint, but it is great for puffy painting with a brush.

Pudding Paint

1   box vanilla instant pudding mix
2   cups ice cold water
       food coloring

Pour pudding mix into a bowl. Add water and whisk. Refrigerate. Separate the pudding into separate containers. Add a couple drops of food coloring to each container. Mix until the color is fully combined.

The colder the water, the better. Lukewarm water makes watery paint.

The paint will continue to thicken the longer you leave it in the fridge.

Pudding Paint will be pastel colored.

Pudding Paint will last a few days at room temperature. After that it will start to spoil.

3 Ingredient Paint

1   cup salt
1   cup all purpose flour
1   cup water
       food coloring

Mix and pour into a condiment bottle to create cheap and easy bottle paint.

1 Minute Play Dough

1   cup all purpose flour
     couple of squirts dish soap
     food coloring

Gradually add dish soap to the flour. Mix and knead until you get the desired consistency. Add a couple drops of food coloring, if desired.

Cloud Dough

1   cup baby oil
8   cups all purpose flour
1   heaping Tbsp. non-toxic tempera paint powder

In a large bowl, stir together the baby oil and flour. Add the tempera paint and stir. Using your fingers, work the dough for several minutes until the color is uniform and the ingredients are soft, silky, and well mixed.

Sand Dough

1   cup shaving cream
⅓   cup clean play sand
⅔   cup cornstarch

Mix all of the ingredients together until the mixture is able to form into a ball.

Molding Clay

½   cup white glue
1   cup cornstarch
     food coloring

Mix. Add a couple drops of food coloring, if desired. Mold. To harden, place in a 200° oven for 1 hour.

Air Clay

1   cup baking soda
¼   cup cornstarch
¾   cup water

Combine the ingredients in a saucepan and stir. Bring to a boil, stirring constantly. Once you see it bubbling, turn it down to about medium and keep stirring until the mixture turns thick and is too hard to mix. This should take about 5-6 minutes. Remove and let it cool in a bowl. Roll out and design as desired. Cover it with plastic wrap while you're working on your cut-outs because it dries pretty quick.

Ocean In A Bottle

     water
     cooking oil
     blue food coloring
     large bottle (2 liter pop bottles work well, mouthwash bottle,
        water bottle)

Fill approximately ⅓ of the bottle with water. Add several drops of food coloring. Fill the rest of the bottle with oil. Put on the lid and twist tightly. Put a piece of tape around the lid so it doesn't come undone. Have your child shake the bottle to disperse the food coloring and watch the ocean form.

Fizzing Sidewalk Chalk

1   cup baking soda
½   cup cornstarch
     warm (almost hot) water
     food coloring

Mix the dry ingredients and then add water, stirring, until it's not too thick. Paint on sidewalk and let dry. It dries quickly. Fill a spray bottle with vinegar. Spray on sidewalk and watch your dried paintings come fizzing to life!

Spray Sidewalk Chalk

1   cup hot water
½   cup cornstarch
1   tsp. washable tempera paint
     squirt dishwashing liquid

Add cornstarch to hot water, whisking to mix so that there are no clumps. Add tempura paint and a squirt of dishwashing liquid. Mix well. Pour it into your squirt bottles and shake well.

After you let your spray sit a while, it will separate. Shake it really well before you use it each time.

Spray down the driveway when you are done to avoid any staining.

Why buy it for $7 when you could make it yourself with $92 of craft supplies?

Paper Mache

2   cups cold water
¾   cup all purpose flour
2   Tbsp. sugar

Boil 1 cup of water in a saucepan. While that is heating up, mix remaining cup of cold water with flour. When water comes to a boil, pour in the flour mixture. Turn heat to medium-high and stir occasionally until it comes to a rolling boil. After boiling, mix constantly for 1-2 minutes, or until it thickens and turns a slightly translucent white.

The paste should be thick but still drip slowly from the whisk. (It will thicken more as it cools.) Turn off heat and mix in the sugar. Let it stand until it cools enough to work with.

This paste can be used in many ways to make basic paper mache forms that can be either left alone or used as a base for other projects.

Homemade Snow

2   boxes (16 oz.) cornstarch
1   can foaming shaving cream

Empty boxes of cornstarch into a box, plastic container, tub, or any other container you have lying around. A container with a lid comes in handy if you want to be able to keep your "snow" to use another day.

Add the shaving cream to the cornstarch. Mix until crumbly and snowy. It will use almost the whole can. If it doesn't stick together enough to make snowballs for snowmen, add a bit more shaving cream.

Bouncy Balls

½   cup warm water
1   Tbsp. borax
1-2   Tbsp. clear glue (or clear glitter glue)

Stir together warm water and borax, until the borax is completely dissolved. (Add more water if it doesn't all dissolve.) If the water is hot, allow it to cool. Next slowly pour glue into the bowl of borax solution. The more glue you use, the bigger the ball! (About 2 tablespoons of glue makes a large ball.)

As soon as the glue hits the borax solution, it will start to harden. Gently squeeze and squish the glue ball until it is no longer sticky.

Remove from the borax solution and roll between your hands to make it ball shaped.

Jello Slime

1   cup cornstarch
1   (3 oz.) box sugar free Jello
½   cup warm water

Combine cornstarch and Jello in a mixing bowl. Mix well.

Slowly mix the water into the mixture (stirring the entire time.) The mixture may become tough to stir as you're adding water. Resist adding extra water, as the consistency will become more like oobleck and less like slime. Continue to stir until the entire ½ cup of water has been evenly incorporated. If you need to add water, add a small drop or two at a time, because the consistency will change quickly.

Play with your prepared Jello slime on a protected surface or tray.
Have fun and ENJOY!

Store Jello slime in an airtight container in the refrigerator for up to a week.

DIY Jelly Soap

½   cup water
1   tsp. salt
1   envelope unflavored gelatin
½   cup liquid soap
    body safe soap colorant*
½   tsp. body safe glitter

In a small pan, bring water to a boil. Add salt and stir.

Empty the packet of gelatin into a small bowl. Add salt and water and stir until gelatin is dissolved. Stir in soap. Add coloring (if desired) and glitter.

Pour mixture into a measuring cup with a spout. Spoon off any froth or bubbles. Place silicone soap molds onto a baking sheet. Pour mixture into soap molds. Refrigerate 2 hours.

*You can use whatever soap you'd like. If you use a colored soap you don't need to add any additional coloring.

*Soap coloring can be purchased at any craft store.

**Silicone ice cube molds can be found in a lot of designs at thrift stores for super cheap!

The longer I stay in the shower, the longer I can pretend that the kids aren't fighting and destroying my house.

Dish Soap Silly Putty

1½   Tbsp. dish soap
2   Tbsp. cornstarch

Mix the dish soap and cornstarch together for about 10 seconds. Then work the mixture until all of the ingredients in the bowl are thoroughly combined. This is when you'll see the putty start to come together.

Because dish soap formulas can vary, it's ok if you need to add a little more soap. If the putty is entirely too dry, add a tiny bit more dish soap to it.

If the putty is too runny, add a tiny bit more cornstarch to it. After adding more of either ingredient, mix the putty by hand for a few moments.

> Some days it feels more like a hostage negotiating with a band of drunken bipolar pirates than actual parenting.

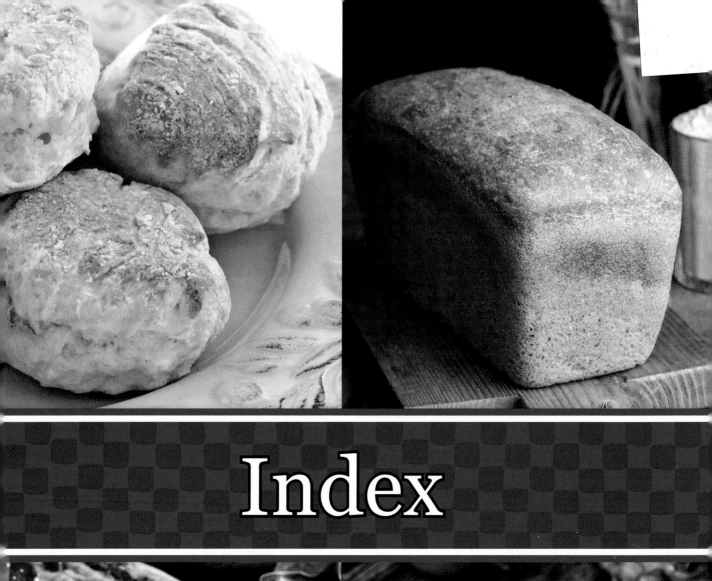

Index

411

Notes

Notes

An Invitation For You

Most people say that coming to a relationship with God is important so that you know where you will go when you die. Really, a relationship with God is so much more than that. It is a relationship with the One who created everything, who created you and who has every desire for your good.

God created us all to be in a perfect relationship with him, but Adam and Eve broke that relationship by turning from Him and breaking that relationship. This is what the Bible calls sin. As a result of that original sin and the sins that we all continue to commit, we are separated from God and hopelessly lost. In His word, God tells us "No one is righteous— not even one" (Romans 3:10) and that a price must be paid for our sin. Unfortunately, the price for our sin is too high for us to ever pay and, without God, we are destined to pay our own price, forever separated from God in what the Bible calls the lake of fire. (Revelation 20:15)

The Good News is that God sent His perfect, one and only Son, Jesus, to pay that price for us. When He died for our sins and rose from the dead, He overcame death and freed us from having to pay our own sin debt, if we are willing to accept His payment for us. It is a free gift (Romans 6:23) that we cannot earn, but that He willingly offers to us. God's desire is not to condemn you (John 3:17), but He will not force you to accept His free gift.

You don't have to be "good enough" to come to Him. God's word says that "while we were yet sinners, Christ died for us" (Romans 5:8). He invites you to come just as you are and promises to make you a new creation and give you eternal life in Heaven with Him. God's word says, "to all who believed him and accepted him, he gave the right to become children of God." (John 1:12)

So how do you accept His free gift?
1) Admit you have sinned.
2) Believe in Jesus, and that He Paid that price for you.
3) Confess that Jesus is Lord and give your life to Him.

You can pray this to Him sincerely in your own words, saying something like, "Dear Lord Jesus, I know that I am a sinner, and I ask for Your forgiveness. I believe You died for my sins and rose from the dead. I turn from my sins and invite You to come into my heart and life. I want to trust and follow You as my Lord and Savior. In Your Name. Amen."

If you do this, God's Word promises that you will be saved, your sins will be forgiven (1 Peter 2:24), and you will spend eternity in Heaven (John 3:16) with the promise that it can never be taken away (John 10:27-28).

If you haven't given your life to Christ, won't you come to Him today?

Got questions? Please feel free to contact us: editor@livingonadime.com